Rose Saunder

Without Let or Hindrance

Dick Powell

To Rose.

Good Luck.

and Best Wishes

Dick Powell

Published by
THE OLD MUSEUM PRESS

Without Let or Hindrance

First published by The Old Museum Press Limited
The Old Museum, Bramber, West Sussex BN44 3WE
England
1997

Cover photograph © Jeremy Irwin

A catalogue record of this book
is available from The British Library

ISBN 1 84042 025 1

Design and typesetting by StewART

Printed and bound in Great Britain by
Biddles Limited, Guildford & Kings Lynn

CONTENTS

To my wife Lil,
for her dedication to my motorcycling
and to my dear friends
Vaclav in the Czech Republic and
the late Hervé le Manach of Brittany.

Grateful thanks to to my friend
Jeremy Irwin who did so much
to get the book off the ground.

INTRODUCTION

I came up with three possible titles for this book but wasn't happy with any of them. Then I remembered an encounter with an East German border guard many years ago. Flicking through my passport, he held it open as he showed it to me and asked what 'without let or hindrance' meant. I plainly told him that it meant 'let me pass', or, more exactly, 'leave me alone.' He almost collapsed with laughter.

He did let me through quickly, though.

Chapter One
BEGINNINGS

It was my latter days at school, in Cheltenham in the 1930s, which proved me with the interest and incentive which was the foundation of my earning a living. Also, mechanically and geographically, it infused me with a sense of adventure.

I was fortunate that our science and engineering teacher was both a find theoretician and a practical man of wide experience. He not only taught us the basics but also gave us the opportunity to put the theory into practice by working on both car and motorcycle engines and equipment, during and after school hours. Indeed, being one of the old school of teachers, he would remain behind long after many had left. Recognising and welcoming our interest and keenness, he would hold impromptu evening sessions. I learned a lot from him.

We also made wireless sets in his classes, starting with the basic crystal set and then progressing to sets with one, two, three or more valves. We built amplifier units with second-hand parts we bought ourselves from wireless repair shops or, as was common in those days, from second-hand furniture shops. We made the wireless cabinets during our woodwork lessons, and any brackets or clips we needed were made during our metalwork lessons. Thus we were always able to see our projects through from the start to the finished, working article.

I started working for a living on my fourteenth birthday. Entering the workshops of a local garage could have been traumatic but for the foundation that school had provided. This both softened the impact for me, and gave me the knowledge, which helped me win the job in the first place.

So, working a minimum of forty-eight hours weekly, I was appointed assistant to a skilled mechanic. He, in order to supplement his weekly wage of £1 10s, would work overtime as often as possible. As an apprentice I was obliged to work with him at all times, but as I was paid by the week it did nothing to improve my income. My wage was two shillings and six pence a week, which would be doubled to five shillings a week for the second year, 7s 6d for the third and 10s for the fourth. Then, at the start of the fifth and final year of apprenticeship, it would double again to a magnificent £1 a week.

Now, this sort of pay would have meant that saving to buy a motorcycle was almost impossible. However, using the skills that I had learned at school, I started taking on repair work in my spare time - bicycles, lawnmowers, agricultural machinery and wireless sets - in an attempt to swell my savings. Thus, my free time was filled with work too. The only riding I was able to do at this time was on motorcycles borrowed from more adult friends, who often believed I was older than I was.

In September 1939, when I was fifteen, the war started. Everything changed dramatically, and along with it went my hopes of buying a motorcycle in time for my sixteenth birthday. Soon, all eligible men were called up for military service. The workers left at the garage were mostly like me, very young, or at the other end of their working lives.

The transformation at the garage was enormous. We had to climb on to the roof and paint over the roof windows with black paint, to block out any light from within in case of bombing raids. Back inside the workshops we had to modify car lights, cutting out cardboard discs to fit inside the head-lamp glass with only a half-circle two inches across cut out in the centre. Sidelights were blacked over, or obscured with more discs permitting only a pinprick of light through a hole of one-eighth of an inch. One-third of the area of a rear lamp was permitted to show, and the lamps illuminating registration plates were completely blacked out. Similar rules applied to motorcycles.

At that time there were many motorcycles made in the 1920s still in daily use. These were fitted with acetylene lighting kits that were quite poor to begin with. The effect of these modifications was to leave virtually no headlamp beam and make night riding on unlit roads quite exciting.

I also remember that bicycles were sometimes fitted with paraffin lamps. In fact this probably became more common during the war because batteries were in such short supply.

The war was also the beginning of the end for the British motorcycle industry. In spite of many critics today who blame the manufacturers themselves, I firmly believed that the industry's heavy commitment to the war effort put them in a serious position when peace returned. After 1945, our governments then failed to back the loyal factories in the same manner as those of the vanquished Germans and Japanese.

My wartime work is another story, but did include much riding on the most common military models made by Matchless, Norton, BSA and Ariel.

Chapter Two
FIRST BIKE

Peace at last. Now it was possible to buy, tax and ride a motorcycle as a civilian. However, many of them had been badly stored during the six years of war and it was quite a problem to find a good buy. But in 1946 I found one, which became my first real bike: a 1935 Douglas Blue Chief in quite good condition.

The Douglas was a bit unusual. It was a twin-cylinder machine of 500cc with the horizontally opposed pistons set 'fore and aft'; that is to say, one behind the other as you sat on the bike. It was air-cooled, and I was told that I could expect the rear cylinder to give trouble due to a lack of cooling air passing over it. In short, it would seize up when very hot.

Sure enough, on my first long ride in the Cotswolds the engine did indeed tighten up. I pulled over, stopped the engine and waited for ten minutes. It had freed off again by this time, so I kick-started it again and rode home slowly with no further trouble.

I soon had the engine out of the frame - quite an easy job on this model - and resting on my workbench. Removing the rear cylinder barrel, I could find nothing wrong at all. So I did the same to the front cylinder, and here I discovered the trouble. The piston rings had seized in their grooves and had very slightly marked the cylinder bore. This puzzled me after hearing so much about the rear cylinder, but I came to the conclusion that it was not heat that had caused the seizure, but lack of oil.

I thought about it some more. I remembered that the engine had tightened at the top of a long, steep climb. The fore and aft cylinder layout meant that the rear one would benefit from the sump oil level at the expense of the front one when the bike was climbing a hill.

Rightly or wrongly, I decided that this was the trouble. So I designed a small cup-shaped component, then drilled and tapped a thread in the crankshaft web to enable me to bolt it in position. My theory was that it would act as a scoop and throw oil on to the front cylinder bore. To my own surprise and the disbelief of others, it worked. I continued to ride the Douglas for the next ten years, the last three with a Swallow sidecar attached, with no trouble whatsoever.

During those years I ran it as a general purpose unit. It had lovely, tractable power that minimised the inconvenience of a hand-change gearbox, as so little gearchanging was required. The engine was also quiet and economical; petrol consumption was about eighty miles to the gallon solo, sixty-five after fitting the sidecar.

I eventually sold this outfit to a man who had pestered me about it for months. Afterwards I wished that I hadn't for he turned the beautiful outfit into a complete wreck inside three months. The sight of it was quite saddening to me.

Chapter Three
FIRST TOURS

I replaced the Douglas with a 1950 Triumph T100 and
Watsonian Avon sidecar after a spell without an outfit. But I
soon separated the pair and ran the bike solo as the low-
octane 'pool' petrol of the time had meant constant
gearchanging to prevent the engine pinking. In the meantime
I had also managed to buy a newish (1948) Ariel VB, a 600cc-
sidevalve single-cylinder machine. I used this for three years
as a main tourer.

In the days of petrol rationing, the acquisition of several
motorcycles was the only was to amass enough coupons to
go touring. A book of coupons issued for each bike added up
to a reasonable amount although the standard ration was
only about two gallons a week, varying a bit according to
size of motorcycle.

I managed to make several trips to Ireland, crossing from
Liverpool to Belfast. My riding in both the north and south
of the Island was hugely enjoyable, in marvellous scenery
and with friendly and sincere people everywhere. I have
returned there frequently ever since. I also took the ferry
from Portsmouth to Le Havre and toured the north of France,

from Calais to Brest. However, I was forced to economise on everything on these holidays as the aftermath of war meant austere living in both countries.

Chapter Four
TURKEY 1949

By 1949 I was planning my first big tour, and with far-off places in my sights I bought a 1936 Matchless G3. This was a single-cylinder 350cc machine, several examples of which I had ridden during the war.

I modernised it by updating the suspension. I fitted some ex-Army telescopic front forks in place of the girder forks. At the rear I fitted the newly invented spring heel. This was made and marketed by G Siddaway of Grantham and was specially made to suit AJS and Matchless. It involved only a slight modification to the existing frame (cutting a small section of the rear wheel spindle slot from it).

The unit consisted of an alloy housing drilled to act as a damping unit, plus support for the spring unit. It used the same spring as the one in the front fork, and was filled with ordinary fork oil. It was bolted on to the frame via the original spindle slots and a sub-frame to the centre frame connecting bolt. The rear wheel was then bolted into the unit and thus was allowed to travel up and down, acting as a spring heel.

It worked, too, and the damping could be adjusted with two spanners at the roadside. It did wear rapidly, though, as the alloy unit sliding up and down over the spring column was alloy to steel. Almost at once Mr Siddaway brought out an improved version that was bushed by phosphorus bronze and supplied with a grease nipple point.

Apart from these modifications, the Matchless was virtually standard. However, to combat the low-octane petrol of the day, I also fitted a compression plate below the cylinder barrel. This had the effect of reducing the compression ratio to about 6:1, enabling the engine to run much better on poor fuel.

My clothing for the trip consisted of a pair of ex-Army trousers, a shirt, pullover, a pair of fireman's waterproof overtrousers and an ex-Army dispatch rider's three-quarter-length coat. My headgear was either a beret or nothing, my footwear the inevitable wellingtons. I also packed some spare underclothes and a pair of shoes.

My camping gear consisted of a small bivouac with loose groundsheet, cotton sleeping bag (ex-Army again), a canvas water bucket, Army mess tin kit, cutlery, enamel mug, water bottle and a small petrol stove. I also took a first aid kit. Spares and tools for the bike consisted of a spark plug, headlamp and tail lamp bulbs, a selection of spanners and screwdrivers and a pair of pliers.

I serviced the Matchless carefully, filled the petrol tank to the brim and took another two gallons in a can. With only £5 in my pocket, but lots of French francs stashed in my luggage from the war, I headed for Dover.

I had already bought my return boat ticket, applying by post to the Dover office. My precious motorcycle was hoisted from the dockside to the deck of the ship. I can still remember seeing it swinging about high above me on the end of a rope. What a contrast to channel crossings today, when one simply rides on to a ferry.

My bike was the only one to go aboard, as indeed it was for most of the trips over the next ten years. It suddenly hit me that I was alone and heading for the unknown. We landed at Calais; I produced the necessary paperwork and made my way northwards to Ostend.

The paperwork in those days consisted of my passport, my driving licence, and a rather huge book of coupons called a *carnet de passage*. On leaving one country to enter another, a coupon was signed surrendered. This was a must: no coupon, no entry (or exit). I also carried an RAC international driving permit issued to me at Calais.

The roads in that part of the world were in a terrible state. The war had left its scars on everything, there were no motorways except in Germany and signposting was virtually non-existent.

It was important to know if the bridges on a proposed route were intact. Many were not, and not knowing which had been destroyed meant having to double back or follow the line of a river or a railway to the next crossing point. This was expensive both in petrol and in time, and I had limited supplies of both. But I had with me some military maps from the war, and these gave a reasonably accurate picture of the main routes. Even after all these years it is probably best not said where I obtained these maps, but they covered France, north and central Belgium and most of Germany.

I seem to remember that the French franc was being exchanged at just under one thousand to the pound. I seldom bought

Belgian francs as the exchange rate varied so much, but in Germany the rate was steady at about eight Marks to the pound. All these numbers could vary a bit anyway, according to how the locals felt, it seemed at times.

Comparison could be made only against value for money, and to get petrol I often traded such things as cigarettes or small bottles of whisky, several of which I had also packed away in my luggage as substitute currency. This sounds a bit risky, but British restrictions meant I had very little money to go as far as I intended.

To make my money go further I also did some work along the way, assisting in repairs to many surplus or abandoned British Army lorries and cars. Sometimes just giving advice was enough, and all I could give anyway as time was tight.

My route took me across Belgium from France, then into Germany, southwards via Frankfurt and Munich, across Austria and into Yugoslavia. I rode from daylight to dusk, then pitched camp at any suitable place - more often than not by the roadside. Mentioning the route like this makes it sound like a simple ride, but at times it was decidedly a dicey business.

I had set myself a schedule of three hundred miles a day. This is not a lot by modern standards, but bear in mind the state of the roads in those days which would occasionally necessitate a delay, or study of my maps and a revision to my route. Finding petrol could also be a problem, although not a big one as the Matchless would cover about three hundred and fifty miles on a tankful, and regularly returned ninety or a hundred miles to a gallon of fuel. The little carburettor, with a bore of only seven-eighths of an inch, was wonderfully stingy!

In that early post-war period, sporting a GB plate was a big help. Time and again I was offered help and kindness by strangers, including being given free food or a tankful of petrol by people who was undoubtedly only just scratching a living themselves in the aftermath of world war. For example, at one point on this trip I decided that I really should change the bike's engine oil. I was in France, on the return leg of the strip. I called in at a garage to see if they stocked Castrol 50 grade. A one-gallon tin of it was produced - curiously, it was a gallon and not five litres. I performed a quick oil change in the street and handed back the half-full tin. My benefactor told me it was a gift and refused to take any money from me.

Or was it the GB plate alone? Perhaps I have been exceptionally lucky over the years, but I prefer to believe that there is something about the solo rider, perhaps his or her very vulnerability, that frequently brings out the best in people.

Continuing south across Yugoslavia, I rode towards the Bulgarian border. At the crossing point at Dimitrovgrad, a rather frightening experience gave me my first challenge of the trip. The Bulgarian border officers declared that my papers, which had taken months to gather together, were not in order. They refused to listen to my protests, and told me that I would be arrested when the security police arrived.

I hadn't realised that they had sent for the police, but come they did. To my astonishment and relief, they took a look at my papers and my bike, and then one of them actually embraced me before sending me on my way towards Sofia. Why they liked me so much I shall never know. One of them spoke almost perfect English, which was quite rare then, so perhaps he had English friends or had even lived or studied here at one time. Unlikely, I admit, but I have no other clues. I rolled through Sofia and Plovdiv and on to the Turkish border.

Conversely, I had no trouble leaving Bulgaria or entering Turkey. It was hardly more complicated than crossing from England to Scotland, and with the Matchless still going well I entered Istanbul and rode over the old bridge in the city centre, the Bosphorus beneath me shining in the intense heat of the day.

Then at last to my chosen port of call: the town of Izmit, and the home of a wartime friend. The real reasons for my ride was to surprise my friend, and to make good a promise I made to visit him after the war. Boy, was he surprised to see me! He almost had to crush me to death to prove to himself that I was real, and kicked my tyres repeatedly to convince myself that the bike was too.

I had covered about three thousand miles, since leaving home on my thirteen-year-old motorcycle. It was behaving itself very well, but I took advantage of the brief respite to check it over. My notes remind me that oil consumption had been almost nil, but that the spark plugs had suffered in burning the poor quality petrol. I fitted my spare one.

My stay was a joyous but very short. Employers offered much shorter holidays then, and after only one night - spent under a roof for a change! - I had to head back home. Money was by now short, as well as time, but I had accumulated some US dollars from a black market source. These could be used almost everywhere, but in my innocence in those days I was never entirely sure of the dollar's value against the local currency, and I probably made some bad deals.

I retraced my route to Salzburg, which took three days, and continued on to Munich and Strasbourg. It was dark when I pitched camp at a makeshift site a few miles into France, but I found a shop still open and bought some food and a bottle of cheap wine. My staple 'on the road' diet was bread, cheese and fresh fruit. When possible I would supplement this with cold meat, and it became quite the norm for the locals to produce tins of British corned beef at the drop of a hat.

The next day I struck camp at five o'clock, kicked the Matchless into life and rode to Paris. Anyone who found themselves in Paris at that time, even up to the late 1950s, would be aware that all its drivers drove with one hand on the steering wheel and the other on the horn-push. Deafened by the noise, if you were not quick enough to get into the road position you wanted, you would be forced or at least intimidated out of the way. On that day I did three circuits of the Arc de Triomphe before I could get into the right lane.

Arriving at Dover, I had a tankful of French petrol, less than £1 in my pocket, about five thousand miles behind me and three hundred more to go.

Telling others about my journey after my return, some thought I was telling some quite untrue story. Those with more information on the Continental situation at that time were amazed that I had managed to find enough petrol, and as comparatively easily as I did.

In any case, this first big foreign trip was to set a precedent. It had given me great confidence both in my Matchless and myself, and the possibilities for future journeys seemed enormous. Many years later I was forcibly reminded of patchy petrol supplies and even more patch roads when I started to visit other, more forbidding parts of Europe, but I will save those stories for later chapters.

Chapter Five
SPAIN 1951

By 1951 my savings enabled me to plan another foreign trip, and this time I decided to head south instead of east. I decided to ride the highest pass over the Pyrenees that I could find, and ride down into Spain with Madrid and Salamanca as possible destinations. I picked the Matchless again for the journey (I also owned the Ariel VB and the Douglas at the time). After all the usual preparations, it was a well-loaded bike that headed off for Portsmouth and the ship for Le Havre.

Once again I had accumulated a fair amount of French francs. This was done with the great help of a seafaring friend who regularly travelled between Dover and Calais. It was all rather illegal but I got away with it. As I was merely returning the money to its country of origin, I could see no wrongdoing - not that I looked very hard for it.

Enough to say that I had a trouble-free run down through France and was soon passing through Toulouse and arriving at the Spanish border near Les. This was a very easy crossing, as the French and Spanish customs officers were most interested in the Matchless and what was described as my 'gigantica load'. But then, they did not know the capability of the bike.

The climb began. As I zigzagged up the tortuous route I soon came to respect the dangerous condition of every bend. Traffic had swept the rubble-strewn surface to the outer edges of the bends - just on the riding line. This was always the most worrying feature and I rode with great caution, but in the end I did make a mistake which could have meant the end of my ride.

I had been keeping an eye on an approaching lorry. I kept getting glimpses of it as the bends unfolded but underestimated its wide load. When we finally met, it was travelling downhill at some speed and filling almost the entire width of the road. I had made a further misjudgement, too, in that we met on a bend. The lorry swept the loose road surface straight at me, some of it shooting from under the front wheels like bullets and peppering me at all points.

I dropped the bike on the gravel on the edge of the road, where I had been forced. I slid off the road over some boulders and down a grass bank to comparatively soft ground. The lorry carried on round the bend and down the mountainside.

Scrambling back up the bank and picking up the bike, I realised that it had fared much better than I had dared to hope. It had keeled over on its left side, but my saddlebags and the luggage packed behind me on the seat had caught on the rocks and stopped it sliding down the hillside. The bags had also cushioned its fall such that the only damage was a bent footrest, and the clutch lever on the left handlebar was knocked out of position.

I was shaken up, but apart from a bruised knee and a cut on my hand I was unhurt. It was a very thankful and obviously much more educated rider who carried on up the twisting mountain road.

I'm not sure of the exact height above sea level that I reached that day. The climb flattened out at around three thousand feet, according to my rather ancient map. The last thousand or so was done in second and third gears as the engine gave notice of its disapproval of the lack of oxygen by always demanding one gear lower than it would at more normal altitudes. It still ran well considering the quality of the petrol and the heavy load it was carrying, but the little carburettor meant that however wide I opened the throttle, nothing more was gained.

I learned to let the engine pull at its own limitations. Decent speeds were out of the question on those roads, anyway.

It was getting dark, so I called a halt of the day and pulled off the road once I had spotted a flattish piece of ground. Pitching my tent soon made me aware that I had hurt myself more than I had realised. Nevertheless, I raised enough energy to bash my damaged footrest back into position.

I made tea and opened a couple of tins to give me the usual corned beef and beans feed. It was dark by the time I finally lay down, peering out of the open end of my tent at my faithful Matchless and the shining stars. I didn't know exactly where I was, except that I was certainly at least several miles from the nearest village. I was a long way from home, I'd had an accident and I ached in one or two places, and yet I felt quite wonderful. It was a feeling that I was to experience many times in the years ahead.

I awoke to find myself shivering, the early morning sun shining on the bike and the vista below. My breakfast was the usual wheat flakes and tinned milk, tea and a slice of now stale bread. As usual, the first kick brought the Matchless to life, and with all my gear safely strapped aboard I began the tortuous, winding climb again.

After only about a mile I reached a customs post. A military-looking gent perused my papers and passport, asked if I had any cigarettes (I hadn't), and then said in French, 'If you are English you had better go!' Only a few years before, German soldiers on the watch for movement out of France must once have manned the post. There was still some barbed wire there, and the best part of the word *Achtung* could be read on a metal sign almost covered in undergrowth.

My ride to Zaragoza was hazardous, the road often degenerating to no more than loose shale, with potholes large enough to wreck my bike and all my plans if I hit them. When I arrived, I tried to change some francs into pesetas but was offered a poor exchange rate, so out came one of my precious US Dollars.

I camped again that night. This time, with a farmer's blessing, I had a beautiful site on the bank of the River Ebro. He also supplied me with bread, cheese and fruit, and what proved to be quite a potent bottle of wine - all free. My luck was in once again, and early the next day I was off on the road to Valencia.

I had not realised how mountainous, remote and beautiful this area was. I could ride for miles without seeing anyone.

I then had a rare encounter with another rider, a Frenchman heading for home. I learned that he had been robbed while camping in the mountains and had lost most of his money. He had done what I had always done, and split his money by hiding some on the bike and some in different items of luggage. However, the two pieces of luggage the thief took, which had been strapped on the top of his load, contained the greater part of his money. His bike, a 500cc Terrot, was quite new and equipped with some lovely leather saddlebags in which he now wished he had hidden his money.

I have heard plenty of hard luck stories over the years. But I believed this man and gave him some of my pesetas and a ten-dollar note. He was quite astonished and nearly crushed me in an embrace. He gave me his address - I remember he lived in Poitiers - and told me to call on him on my return journey. As events turned out I never did, but like to think that he remembered that day from time to time as I do and perhaps thought better of the English because of it.

Valencia was a busy port and full of people, but not really to my taste. Besides which I was up against the clock as usual. To keep to my schedule I knew I must get under way. I camped again that night - no free food this time - and set off early for Madrid, a ride of two hundred and twenty miles. I rode west through mostly flattish countryside by way of Motilla del Palancar and Tarancón and, in blistering heat, reached the outskirts of the city.

It was here that I met a most friendly gentleman; it was this chance meeting that really 'made' my trip for me. Sat on the bike and contemplating the busy city traffic, I didn't hear his Mercedes pull up behind me. He got out, walked up and asked if I was all right. This gave me quite a start, but this charming manner soon put me at my ease. Yes, I replied. I was just wondering which way to go.

His reply, and in English too, was 'Then I shall make up your mind for you. Please follow me. 'We turned off the main road and headed south along a pleasant, quiet tree-lined road. I wondered where I was going and for at least ten miles I shadowed this big saloon car, the driver occasionally waving out of the window to reassure me of his intentions.

Then he swung off the road and up a beautifully kept driveway towards an equally magnificent house, and around

25

the rear to a flagstoned courtyard. My new friend jumped out of his car, opened two great doors to the building on my left and beckoned me inside. Placing the Matchless on the prop stand - with the bike loaded up I could never find the strength to use the main stand - I gazed in wonder at a whole row of neatly arranged motorcycles. 'My collection,' he announced. 'But more of them later. Come, you must wash and eat.'

By now I was really puzzled, but also very pleased. After a luxurious bath and shave, my first for several days, I found myself sat at an immense polished table literally groaning with the weight of food and wine.

'How rude of me,' he said. 'I forgot to mention, my name is José.' I told him mine, and the next question was over where I lived. When I told him of Cheltenham and the Cotswolds, I was amazed to learn that he knew it! He had been at Cheltenham College from 1936 to 1939, and his father had also been to school in England. We talked freely about the area, and well into the night, pausing only to eat and drink. Some evening!

The next day, at breakfast, he asked me if I had time to stay another night so that we could go to a motor club meeting nearby. I have long made it a rule that, while I sketch out an itinerary for each trip, I don't stick to it if an interesting diversion presents itself. Part of the pleasure of travelling, and particularly of travelling alone, is that these unexpected incidents crop up. They should not be turned down in order to keep to a timetable. So I agreed, and we went out to inspect his collection.

They were mostly BMWs, ranging from a very early model which I think was a Helios with BMW's M2B15 proprietary engine (a flat twin), and also a Victoria with the same 500cc engine and chain drive. There was a 1923 R32, which would be

26

worth a fortune today as the model was the first complete motorcycle which BMW made, and an R16, which was a 750cc flat twin. Most interesting to me was a marvellous example of a BSA 250cc sidevalve ' Round Tank' model from about 1924. This bike was like new. José started it and invited me to ride it up and down his long driveway. Then there was a Norton, again 1924, a 490cc overhead valve model, and a Norton CS1 with overhead camshaft from 1930.

We then turned our attention to my faithful steed, which suddenly looked rather dusty and well-travelled next to this gleaming collection. I explained that it was a 1936 model, updated in a few areas. He was quite astonished when I told him of my travels and was impressed by the quietness of the engine and gearbox.

Any motorcyclists reading this will forgive me for a moment while I jump on a favourite hobbyhorse. It is a longstanding joke amongst riders, some of whom have never owned one, that British bikes are all unable to keep their oil on the inside. I don't know how or when this particular story began, but José's remark and my diaries show that it was a long time ago! Perhaps I have been lucky, or perhaps I treat my bikes more considerately than average, but I can honestly say that I have never found my bikes to be inherently leaky.

Anyway, I was allowed to ride the CS1 to the meeting while José rode the OHV model, a basketful of food and wine bottles strapped precariously to the rear carrier. We rode for twenty miles along narrow, twisting roads and tracks until we came up to a small village, the name of which I no longer remember. There was a large gathering of cars and bikes in the central square. Our arrival caused quite a stir and my hand was nearly detached from my arm as I was introduced to and shook hands, with all and sundry.

The day's event proved to be more of a social, eating and drinking occasion than a motor meeting, but was none the worse for that. It was most interesting to study the old cars from many parts of Europe, most of which no longer have car industries. Amongst the bikes there were the inevitable BMWs, a nice Belgian Sarolea 350 (I had never seen one before), a French René - Gillet, and two BSAs from 1920-30. The only reason I can name them after all this time, is that I jotted down details on the back of my old map of Spain. Today, the only scrap of the map which remains is that part with the list on it.

By late afternoon, it was a somewhat wine-affected pair who kick-started their bikes and thundered out of the village. With no question of breath tests then, we certainly made those Nortons gallop on the way home! There followed another night of dining and, I am sorry to say, more wining, followed by too deep a sleep which meant that I started my ride home later in the day than usual.

As I prepared to leave, it occurred tome for the first time that I had not seen anyone in the house except José's two servants. I never did ask him how he came to be living alone in his grand house. Just before I left he presented me with two badges for my bike, one with Calella marked on it, and the other engraved Real Automovil Club Espana.(RAC) I still have them, although I never truly knew the significance of either, or José's connection with them.

The extra day and night I had stayed meant that I could afford only a quick ride around Madrid before heading north-west to Salamanca, a route which again was across mountains and, as it turned out, on bad roads in places. With a large food supply donated by José, I paused only for a brief lunch during the day's ride. He had also emphatically refused to accept any money, so I had plenty for petrol and made up my mind to pass on through Salamanca and head for the Embalse de Almendra, a finger-shaped reservoir about twenty miles long that leads nearly to the Portuguese border.

In sticky afternoon heat, I found a place to camp at the point where the River Esla pours into the reservoir. This was cooler, but had the disadvantages of squadrons of mosquitoes and what seemed in the silence like a huge noise from the river.

I camped on the north side of the lake, so in the morning I rode up to the border along a small valley until I came to the River Duero, which also serves as the borderline. Following what was no more than a track, I finally came out on the road to Zamora, then a smoother ride up to Benavente, hardly seeing a soul. Maybe it was the heat keeping people indoors; it must have been close to a hundred degrees. But the Matchless still ran on, and after a drink in a cantina I headed for Leon and a rather less pleasant experience.

Leon, a fairly large town at the foot of the Cordillera Cantabrica Mountains, seemed to be full of tourists. At least, that was the impression I got as many people asked me for directions to places unknown to me.

I decided to stay for the night in a small hotel on the outskirts, but was a little worried about leaving the bike out in the road overnight. However, the hotel owner assured me that it was 'OK senor, all OK.' I didn't particularly believe it, so, beginning to wish that I had camped instead, I unloaded the bike and lugged everything into my room, then made sure I could see it from the window. I dragged a large upright chair in front of the window and sat in it, looking into the street.
I must have dozed off then, but was suddenly woken up by a crash outside. I could see two shadowy figures standing over my bike, trying to heave it upright. I had been awoken by the sound of it falling over.

There was no time to unlock my door and run down the passage to the front door. I leapt straight out of the window - my room was on the ground floor, but it was still a drop of several feet - and ran towards them shouting all sorts of abuse. It must have given them a fright because they both fled and disappeared in the darkness, leaving me standing over my fallen Matchless. It had been on the main stand for once, and they must have lost control of it as they rolled it off the stand. From what I could see in the ark, the only damage was a snapped clutch lever.

By this time I had been joined by the proprietor of the hotel, who then allowed me to wheel it into the comparative safety of this front garden. He was most apologetic, to the point of becoming quite annoying as he repeatedly told me how such a thing had never happened before. Indeed, the more he insisted, the less I believed him, so when I got away from him and back to my room I remained awake and watching for the rest of the night.

My breakfast was as disappointing as the rest of my night's stay. I went out to inspect the bike again, and confirmed that the broken lever was the only damage. Luckily I had taped a spare to the bike's frame. Some years before, and much nearer home, my bike had been knocked over in a car park and snapped a lever in the same way, and so I had taken this precaution every since. Fitting the spare took five minutes.

I paid my hotel bill reluctantly because everything had been below par, but I could only blame myself for not taking note of the several warning signs: lots of tourists, the dishevelled appearance of the hotel itself, the owner whom I disbelieved. In fact, as I went in to pay, I was sure that the two lads talking to him in the bar were the same two I had frightened off a few hours before. But I left a little wiser. This, after all, was just another experience that would be of use to me for future travels.

I took the road to Riano through quite hilly terrain. However, in the main, the road followed the river valley through some really lovely country. When I arrived in Riano I stopped and made some tea beside a lake. That certainly went down well after the terrible coffee I had been given at the hotel. I continued on towards the north coast and Santander, a busy port full of fishing and pleasure boats, and on towards Bilbao. Here I found a campsite that was more of the style found today. I bought food and a bottle of good wine in the little shop there, so relieving myself of my usual cooking operations.

Time was now running very short, so I was off early the next morning with Bordeaux as my target for the day. I rode through San Sebastian, had only a ten minutes delay at the French border, passed Biarritz and was in Bordeaux by mid-afternoon. So I decided to carry on and finally camped a little to the north of Angoulême, in a field that I shared with a few cows.

Before it grew dark the Matchless was checked over first by the cows and then by me. None of us could find anything worth mentioning, and I made up my mind to make another early start and hope to ride right up to Le Havre. This I did, buying petrol in Poitiers while reluctantly deciding I would not call on the Terrot rider crossing the Loire at Tours, then on to Orleans, bypassing Paris through Versailles, Rouen, and at last into Le Havre.

Soon my Matchless was swinging on the end of a rope, upwards and on to the deck, and the final stage of another journey had been reached.

It was raining in Portsmouth. The bike started up at once and I arrived back in Cheltenham mid-afternoon. It was at the very moment of arriving home that a funny thing happened. As I rolled to a halt outside my house, another rider stopped alongside. He was very young, and at a glance at his bike showed that he had also been touring. He looked at my machine and asked if I was moving house. Before I could answer, he pointed out that his bike was less heavily loaded but that he had been on a big trip - camping, in Wales. But then, he said, I have a new bike so I can make a trip like that.

I never explained. After all, everyone has to start somewhere, and I have often found it difficult to convince prospective Continental travellers that you do not need a new bike or a big bike to make a long journey. This trip had taken twelve days and I had covered 3,100 miles without any mechanical problem. Luck had been on my side as usual, I had met mainly good people who put up with my bad Spanish and French, and I had ridden some wonderful roads and seen some wonderful sights for the first time.

As it turned out, that was to be my last trip as a lone motorcyclist for some time. During the following years and up to 1973 my wife Lil would usually accompany me, sometimes as a pillion passenger, more often as a sidecar passenger.

Chapter Six
MORE BIKES

By 1957 my touring and general purpose bike was a 1955 Matchless G80. This was a similar machine to my pre-war 350, but, being a 500 and benefiting from twenty years' development, was a still more comfortable and practical long-distance mount. On the debit side it was a little thirstier, but only a little.

I was the bike's third owner, having bought it in a rather wrecked condition. I rebuilt it with new big end and mains, rebored the cylinder and polished the cylinder head, and I remember that the purchase price and the cost of parts came to £42. I have done this many times over the years: buying a neglected or high-mileage bike, making it roadworthy and then either selling it on at a small profit or keeping it for my own use.

I ran it on standard carburettor settings and a piston with an 8:1 compression ratio. I used a slightly oversize 4.00 x 19-inch rear tyre and standard gearing, and the bike would return a good eighty miles per gallon on super or four-star petrol at a steady sixty miles an hour. I used hydraulic oil in the front forks and 30-grade engine oil in the primary case and the rear suspension units.

Some examples of parts life: rear chains lasted 45,000 miles, primary chains about 80,000. A front tyre would last for 30,000 miles, a rear one 20,000. Oil consumption: nil. I changed the single spark plug every 10,000 miles.

The Matchless wasn't my only bike, for by this time I had managed to build up a small collection in the way that many motorcyclists do. I still had the Triumph T100 (a sporty 500cc twin-cylinder, twin-carb machine), a very fast Excelsior Manxman and a little BSA C10, so it was a mixed bag.

I had another BSA, too: an M21 with an Avon sidecar fitted. This big, single-cylinder bike was already looking rather dated by 1957, but could still be seen being ridden by AA patrolmen of the day. Its predecessor, the M20, had been turned out in huge numbers for the forces during the war, like my earlier Matchless 350.

I hadn't been riding the M21 long before I noticed that the engine appeared to run rather hot. Checking that the fuel/air mixture, valve and ignition timing were all spot on made no difference. Although the bike had only 4,000 miles or so on the clock at the time, I took it off the road and removed the cylinder head and barrel for examination.

I couldn't find anything very disturbing, so I decided to work on the porting of both the inlet and exhaust tracts. This meant smoothing out the passageways and taking off some of the harsh, jutting-out area immediately below the valve seats. This was hardly 'tuning' in the usual sense of the word, for the M21 was the very opposite of a sports motorcycle. Its power output was modest and its top speed low, but it was a gutsy slogger ideally suited to pulling a sidecar. I was simply trying to make the best of what I had.

I followed up this work by polishing the ports by hand with emery paper, finishing with Brasso on a small circular buff. I ground the valves in well and, on reassembly, gave the exhaust valve at least 0.002 inches more clearance than recommended.

The transformation was fantastic. The BSA pulled better and ran cooler, and a bonus was quite an improvement in fuel consumption. It had previously given me about fifty miles to the gallon with the sidecar fitted; this now jumped to over sixty.

Chapter Seven
HERVE LE MANACH

I met Hervé when I was riding from my home in Braunton (we had moved to north Devon in 1954) to Barnstaple on my Ariel Red Hunter, a beautiful little machine of 250cc made in 1939. He was riding an ex-Army Royal Enfield and gave me a wave as we passed, Hervé heading towards Braunton. On my return journey an hour later, we passed on the road again, but this time we both stopped for a word.

Hervé soon explained that he was on a student exchange, learning to be a teacher at the technical school. He was only eighteen years old but his English was already quite good, he was full of life and, to my surprise, very knowledgeable about most makes of machines. He was most interested in the Ariel, and when I invited him to my home to see my other machines, he accepted and so our friendship began.

I introduced him to our local bike club and over the following months prior to his return to France, and we made many trips together. Of course, an invitation to do the same thing around his home in Brittany soon followed. They were great times. Hervé's family were delightful people and his range of contacts in the motorcycle world was quite amazing.

In 1979 I took Hervé on my 1963 AJS 350 (of which more later) on his first Dragon Rally. This is a camping weekend held in deepest Wales in deepest winter. It is firmly established in the motorcyclist's rallying calendar, and Hervé's visit gave him the incentive to repeat the visit with French friends on many more occasions. I have very fond memories of those occasions.

Our house was his second home and he stayed with us on innumerable occasions. He liked to see me demonstrate the correct way to make tea, boiling water and putting the milk in the cup first. Sometimes, in France and in my company, he would demonstrate this technique to an erring fellow countryman.

Hervé soon acquired a Vincent Rapide and became quite an expert on the marque. He joined the Vincent HRD Owners Club in Britain and came to know another French owner, also called Hervé and also living in Brittany. Between them they designed and modified parts for Vincents and made many friends in the club.

More recently, we rode together to the FIM rally in Barcelona. I entered Hervé as a member of the British contingent, met him at his home, and we went over the Pyrenees again on his Vincent and my AJS.

Tragically, Hervé died of a heart attack in 1990 at only thirty-four years of age. This was a great surprise, as he was a young man in the prime of life. I attended the funeral and it was as clear to see that his family, his many friends and his pupils at the school where he taught were as upset as I was. He was the kind of man who stays in the memory - always in a hurry as he had so many friends to see - always the smiling gentleman.

Hervé had acquired a few other motorcycles by the time he died, including an AJS and a Moto Guzzi Falcone, although his real love remained the Vincent marque. Hervé's parents gave me his 1969 BMW R60 in memory of our friendship. I have re-registered it and so have something solid and rideable to remind me of him whenever I ride it.

Chapter Eight
SCOTLAND 1973

In the last chapter I mentioned my Ariel. The capability of this pre-war machine was well illustrated in 1973. The stage was set at the Ariel Owners Club's annual rally, held that year at Caddington, when some unbalanced person said to the gathering in the beer tent that somebody had said that no road bike could cross the Corrieyairack Pass. We all chorused, 'Of course, Ariels would.' Then, following an acute silence, someone else asked, 'Corriey what?' and 'Where is it?' It was explained that the pass was a military road, built by General Wade during the Scottish wars. It rose to about 2,600 feet above sea level and was very rocky.

Perhaps as you would expect, in a beer tent at a rally, several of us said we could and would do it. Perhaps more surprisingly, none of us later had second thoughts, and a few weeks later eight Ariels and one Velocette converged from various parts of Britain on the lovely town of Dalwhinnie. It was six hundred and fifty miles of September sunshine and showers for me, but my little Ariel didn't miss a beat all the way.

All nine of us stayed the night in a hotel in Dalwhinnie and planned our campaign. We decided that it would be best to start early and ride around to the north end of the pass. This meant we would be nearer our base at the finish. Thus, at around eight o'clock in the morning we set out on our very enjoyable run, arriving at our starting point on the general's famous road. To understand better what the ride was like, think of it not as a road but a track, although even that is charitable.

Before leaving home I had thought about this and fabricated a sump guard from a piece of sheet metal one-eighth of an inch thick. Then I fitted a rear tyre four inches wide in place of the standard 3.25 - there was just enough room. The Ariel's ground clearance was normally less than five inches, with the only lightweight frame Ariel had made at that time. The bigger tyre increased clearance by over an inch. Having girder forks also meant that on full deflection, ground clearance was reduced. With aluminium engine cases, I had to err on the side of caution.

I need not have worried. The Ariel proved it had the heart of a lion and the frame of an elephant. All nine of us set off along the rutted track, thinking that it wasn't so bad after all. But after less than two miles it grew steeper and the surface changed to loose stone and rocks. By the time I had covered five miles I was well up in the mountains and the group had became rather separated. I was still in the lead with George Penny from Hampshire close behind, but there was no sign of the others.

George and I stopped and five stragglers joined us. Bob Brassington, a northern rider of great repute, volunteered to go back to find out what had happened, and Alan Verrall volunteered to wait for him. So it was four Ariels and the Velocette that carried on up the pass. I took the lead again, and could feel the wind gathering strength as we gained height.

It was now a matter of bashing over the rocks, some of which were by now over a foot in diameter. That, coupled with the steepness of the climb, gave us no time to enjoy the views. As we ploughed on up towards the clouds, the mist obscuring almost everything, I braked to a halt in front of two immense rocks. I thought, shall I go left or right? Both seemed dangerous, and I was still trying to make up my mind when the two rocks got up and staggered off. They were large shaggy-coated sheep.

On I went, wrestling with the Ariel sometimes, hauling it off great rocks and noticing with surprise that I could ride it with the clutch fully engaged virtually all the time, so well did the little engine pull. More by instinct than certainty, I at least came to a halt on what I thought must be the summit. Above the howling wind I could just make out the sound of another single-cylinder machine getting nearer. It was George.

About ten minutes later along came Alan and Bob, Colin Craig and Dick Henry on his Velo, along with Roy, our local host, and Dave close behind. Poor old Dick had holed the crankcase of his Velo; not a big hole, but enough to allow oil to seep out. Almost everyone had dented silencers, and my homemade sump guard had been beautifully shaped by the rocks to the exact profile of the crankcase.

A small ceremony took place, with the pre-arranged handing over of a big end assembly from one rider to another. It sounds a bit daft, but then what were we doing up there anyway?

We started the descent, again riding into driving mist. I soon found myself alone again at the front of the line, and facing a solid-looking gate ten feet wide. I half-carried the bike to one side of it, and then realised that the fence on either side of it had long since rusted away, so I rode past the gate and continued downwards.

It really was hairy. The gradient grew steeper and steeper, with water running down the track making the rocks slippery. My brakes became useless as the lining became soaked, and I started to make heart-stoppingly-fast progress completely involuntarily. At last, and about eighteen miles from the start. I came upon the better-surfaced exit track. Looking behind I saw George not far off and still in one piece, and he was soon followed by the others.

Back at our hotel the talk was all of our individual experiences. Poor Mick Stroud, who had failed to make the first part of the road, had suffered irreparable clutch slip. Roy had aborted his effort to help Mick, but seven bikes had conquered the Corrieyairack and that was a fact.

What was funny was how they all mentioned the gate in the middle of nowhere. I realised that I had been the only one to notice that there was no fence there. Every one of them had dismounted, opened the gate, remounted, ridden through, dismounted, shut the gate, remounted and continued!

The next day George and I rode home together for most of the way. For every one of the fourteen hundred miles, plus the battering it received on the pass, my lion-hearted Red Hunter had filled me with pride and admiration.

Chapter Nine
CZECHOSLOVAKIA 1974:
TRAVELLING IN COMPANY

In January 1974 I saw a small article in the magazine of the AJS and Matchless Owners Club which grabbed my interest. Later that year there was to be a rally for four-stroke motorcycles in Czechoslovakia, and entries from Britain were invited.

I thought this would be very interesting so I wrote to the organiser, Vaclav Hamsik, to tell him that I would like to attend. I discovered that four other club members had had the same idea, and the five of us agreed to meet at Ramsgate and travel together.

To step back in time for a moment, preparations for the trip reminded me of an incident in 1961. It hadn't meant much to me at the time, but the implications of it dogged me no end. I had been visiting a friend in the Netherlands. He lived close to the German border in the small town of Winschoten, and he suggested a ride to Berlin to spend a day with a friend of his. We crossed into Germany without much trouble and went on to Hanover, Magdeburg, and Brandenburg, then under the great gateway arches and into Berlin.

As we passed the Brandenburg Gate we noticed construction work in progress but couldn't see what it was. Our friend in

43

Berlin worked for the city council and he knew only too well. The Wall was going up. He told us to leave as quickly as possible, as all aliens would soon be held for questioning. There was some delay at the border this time, but in the end the German guards seemed relieved to be getting rid of us.

This was really my first adventure on the G80 and, looking back on it, I see that it was quite historic. A really solid bit of the Iron Curtain, and an infamous wall that split Berlin in two.

But back to 1974 and Ramsgate docks, where five club members congregated on two AJS 350cc models, a Matchless G9, a G11 and my G80. Landing at Calais, and with it being assumed that I was the most experienced Continental traveller amongst us, I was appointed leading on the road. I decided to use only a limited amount of French motorway, none in Germany, and to follow the Rhine down to Bonn on ordinary, good roads.

We experienced a rare sight on entering Bonn. There was a great show of strength on the part of both the police and the military, and thousands of people milling about in the streets. Finally we were stopped and made to wait by the roadside in the city centre, in the midst of a great crowd. None of us knew what was going on so I asked a spectator. I was told that Marshall Tito was to visit the city and would shortly pass down that very street. Which he did, preceded and followed by an armada of military and police vehicles.

It was staggering to see the immense precautions that were taken but then again perhaps not, when you remember that Yugoslavia was the first country to rebel against Communist occupation and remember how Tito was becoming respected in the West at the time.

It was at least two hours after the cortege had passed before we were able to get on our bikes and make headway out of

44

Bonn, and this was when one of our party made a simply mistake which could nevertheless have been fatal, humorous though it was.

Dear old Stan, a most loveable character, suddenly passed me for no reason at all and took the lead as we approached a roundabout. He forgot we were abroad and went round it the wrong way, somehow missing dozens of cars as he did so. Exiting the roundabout he carried straight on, riding along on the right-hand side of the road as if nothing had happened.

About sixty miles later on we stopped for a rest and, as casually as I could manage, I asked him, 'Stan, what happened at the roundabout back there?' The reply, 'What roundabout?', had the rest of us in stitches for some reason. He looked at us all as if we were mad, which of course only made it funnier.

After a night in a pleasant small hotel in Waldorf, we rode to the border at Rozvadov. We passed through the German control and rode across two hundred yards of no-man's land to the first barrier of the Czech border post. I had crossed similar borders before by my companions had not, so were impressed in various ways by the heavily armed guards and the slow and deliberate way they carried out their task. I will discuss the ins and outs on Eastern European Border crossings later, but every one is different and negotiating them in a minimum time is an art and a science.

This time it took the five of us two hours, after which we rode on to Plzen and finally reached Prague, making our way slowly along we me desperately trying to identify the landmarks I had been given. I had agreed to meet a friend in Prague at half-past four that afternoon, at a rendezvous described in a letter. To complicate matters, this friend was only a pen friend at that time. I had come to know him through the magazine of the Ariel Owners Club.

Finally I decided that we were at the rendezvous. I stopped, turned off the engine and said confidently to the others, 'This is the spot. It's four o'clock, so we have a half-hour wait.'

Half-past four arrived and everyone looked at me expectantly. Then, above the din of the traffic in the street, I could make out the steady beat of a four-stroke single. Into view came our host on a much-modified Ariel. Frank Svata has remained a friend to this day, and I was relieved to see him for this first time. Normally I am a lone rider, responsible only to and for myself.

There were introductions and handshakes all round, and then we followed Frank through the traffic and over many tram-lines to his flat. Well, not exactly to his flat as it was on the second floor, but into an old courtyard, clanging the great doors shut behind us. We were thus able to leave the bikes in comparative safety, flanked by the high walls of the surrounding buildings. This was indeed one of the older parts of Prague.

We were then all introduced to Frank's wife, Jana. Were they pleased to see us! Frank later told me that he did not think we would come. But there we were, in the middle of Communist controlled Czechoslovakia.

Frank's English was very good and a great night was spent talking motorcycles and what was happening in England. It was then that the limitations of existence in the country became more obvious. Jana brought us the only coffee they had, a poor Turkish concoction in which the spoon would stand vertically in the middle of the cup. Stan was having a good holiday: he never forgot the mouthful of sandy substance he swallowed, tipping the cup too far as he drank. For years after, Frank referred to all drinks of uncertain virtue as 'Stan's coffee'. Such is the humour of most Czechs I have met.

We learned that two other Prague motorcyclists were going to the Four-Stroke Rally, so we contacted them and they volunteered to lead us, as they knew the way. As it turned out, they didn't know the way at all. They were also unaware of the stringent laws existing at that time in their own country.

We were only about four miles out of Prague when to our surprise we caught two other British riders. Both on Matchless twins, they were riding very slowly. We overtook and then stopped to see if all was well. They said that they were riding slowly because they had fallen foul of the law by exceeding fifty miles an hour on the main road. Carry on, they said, and we'll see you at the rally.

On we went towards Brno, and this was where my experience paid off. As we dipped down into a village I spotted a police car ahead. I could tell that the Czech rider in front of me hadn't seen it. I dropped down into third gear and stormed past him, accelerated past the police car and the two policeman standing in the road, and swept up the hill out of the village as far as possible. I looked behind - no bikes in sight - so rode on for about another mile, then pulled off the road into the cover of some trees.

At least an hour went by before I heard the sound of bikes approaching, so I left my cover and flagged down some very forlorn riders. They had been fined for speeding. My behaviour maybe hadn't helped, but it would have been impossible for the policemen to have judged the bikes' speeds anyway. So it was just a trumped-up charge, but I really knew that this did not matter. You never argued the law in Eastern Europe; you just paid up.

Feeling slightly guilty, I rejoined the group and we rode on. Apparently it had cost them a hundred crowns each (about £5 at the time), and no doubt had greatly improved their eyesight.

Passing through Brno, we turned onto a more minor road, which to me seemed to be taking us in the wrong direction. We had ridden about a hundred and fifty miles since leaving Prague and had split into two groups, each led by a Czech, and I was becoming increasingly worried about the direction we were taking.

Finally I stopped our leader and challenged him. He agreed that he was lost, so I studied his map and worked out where we were. I estimated we were still eighty miles from the rally site and well off course, and it would soon be dark. He seemed pleased when I said I would lead; a few miles later I noticed that we had lost the group following us, but remembered that they too had a map and thought it best to carry on.

With me was Stan on his G9 and our Czech friend on a 500cc Norton ES2 of 1964 vintage, so with my G80 we were able to travel at a reasonable rate. Then big raindrops began to fall, and just as we arrived at the rally site at Story Horezecov at about ten o'clock, the rain just belted down, accompanied by thunder and lightening. At that instant all the lights on the campsite went out. Torches and candles were produced as we abandoned our bikes and ran for cover. At least we were lucky to have made it before the worst of the storm.

Even apart from the weather, our reception can only be described as fantastic. Vaclav Hamsik, the organiser, was beside himself with pleasure at our arrival. Everyone wanted to meet us and make us welcome. I'll never forget that night. Soon the lights came back on and we went out to the bikes, wheeling them down to the chalets we had been given and partly unpacking before throwing ourselves down on the bunks and wondering where the others were.

It was two in the morning and we were half-asleep when we heard the others ride in. They had become hopelessly lost and nearly drowned in the storm.

The next day we were able to appreciate the size of the rally and the extent of the international presence. Wandering around the site we could see bikes and riders from Germany, the Netherlands, Sweden, Denmark and Poland, and several more from adjoining Eastern Bloc countries. But when we asked about the two other British riders we had seen the previous day, we were told that they hadn't arrived. Two other British riders did arrive that morning, however, one on a Velocette and Dave Pope, the secretary of the Norton Owners Club, on a Commando.

I gradually found out just how difficult it had been for Vaclav to stage the rally at all. It was greatly frowned on by the authorities, and in fact a few years later it was made illegal. But for the next three days we made short trips out of the site on the bikes, and there was much bike talk and humour as the various nationalities struggled to make themselves understood.

The rally had been organised by the newly formed Ctyr Takt Klub (Four-Stroke Club) of Czechoslovakia, but it soon became the International Four-Stroke Club after the success of this first event. I still have a trophy of those times, which brings back many memories whenever I look at it. It is a lovely hand-turned wooden pot bearing the name of the rally and that of the nearest town and Vaclav's home, Bojkovice.

The good-byes came, and Stan and I set off together for the FIM Rally, an annual event being held that year in Austria. This too is a great event but is also another story.

From there we rode as hard as we could, while keeping to the strict Austrian limits of twenty-eight miles an hour in villages and under fifty in the country. We reached the border late in the afternoon and went through the usual performance and two hours later we were on a campsite in West Germany.

The next morning we had a straightforward ride to Aachen, where we camped for the night, intending to make an early start for Calais. However, by this time Stan's bike had developed a petrol leak and we had an early delay, waiting for Aachen's petrol stations to open.

After refuelling, Stan took off before I was quite ready and disappeared. I assumed he was still ahead of me when I reached the border, so I kept going into Belgium and then France. I reached Calais at around noon, still not having seen him since first thing that morning. I was quite worried but couldn't do anything about it, so I rode onto the hovercraft and was soon riding out of Ramsgate.

Such are the perils of travelling with others.

I eventually discovered the fate of the other two Matchless riders (brothers, as I later found out) we had come across in Czechoslovakia. Just after we left them they had stopped again, but had made the big mistake of doing so in a military zone. They were arrested almost immediately and taken to a police station. Their luggage was searched and questions asked about their destination. Being inexperienced in Eastern European travel, they had innocently replied that they were going to a motorcycle rally.

Anyway, a few brass ornaments they had bought on their way east were described by the secret police as possibly being gold. The brothers spent the night in jail until an English-speaking shopkeeper was brought in to translate and they were at last released. They were so disgusted with their treatment, having had to pay another fine to be released that they decided to turn around and go straight home. So, no rally for them, and they swore never again to cross the border into an Eastern Bloc country.

Stan finally made it home, but apparently he had set off the wrong way after buying petrol and rode many miles before the rising sun told him he was heading east.

Chapter Ten
EASTERN BLOC CUSTOMS

To take a motorcycle behind the Iron Curtain in those days meant jumping through a series of administrative hoops. It was an excessively bureaucratic affair, and I often wondered if discouragement was part of the reason for it.

First I would apply to the appropriate Embassy in London for a visa application form. This usually had to be filled out in quadruplicate and meant almost signing my life away. I would spend an evening ploughing through all these forms and send them back with at least four passport-type photos, my passport and a cheque. Weeks would go by and then back would come a visa, my passport stamped by the embassy, a paper for the bike, and more papers to enable me to exchange British money for the country's currency. New and very clean money notes were a must, and for Czechoslovakia, only the £1 notes of the time were accepted. I always assumed this was due to a fear of forgeries.

If I wanted to stay in East Berlin I had to buy a further document from the Westminster Bank. This paper had to go to Berlin along with my explanation for wanting to visit and maybe stay for a while. There would follow a three-month wait, when I would receive this approved document back along with a visa to visit East Germany. These, together with my passport and a paper for the bike, then went to the London Embassy for approval, which took another month.

Whenever I stayed with my friend in East Berlin I had to go to the 'street controller' and write down my personal details in his book, explaining why I was there. As the years went by I seemed to be the only person making any entries in this book. I wish I could have taken it somehow after the fall of the Wall.

For Poland, Hungary, Albania, Yugoslavia and Romania the details differed but the procedures were much the same. In Poland I was supposed to buy petrol coupons at the border, but I never did. My preferred strategy was to wait for a time when a petrol station was quiet. The attendants always seemed pleased to fill an Englishman's tank and appreciated my tact in not letting them be seen serving me.

I felt it important to bear I mind at all times when travelling behind the Iron Curtain that, as far as the authorities were concerned, I wasn't welcome. Amongst the people of the country, starved of contact with the decadent West, it was quite the opposite. But even being seen talking to a Westerner could lead to trouble if seen by the police or a police informer.

When border guards were operating in pairs, as they often were, I would present myself to the older man whenever possible. I soon realised that the younger a guard was, the more zealous and unpleasant he was likely to be, having been brainwashed from entry into the service. The older man would often offer apologies for the inconvenience whilst looking over his shoulder at his colleague, who was always keeping an eye on him. They would say to me, 'So sorry, but I have to do this.' Sometimes they would show their contempt for their own system by looking at my passport and papers while holding them upside-down, merely going through the motions for the sake of appearances.

Other were more corrupt. I can bring to mind an incident at Checkpoint Charlie in Berlin when, after all the preliminary control checks and examinations had been made, I got the bike and myself to the barrier. Here I was ordered to park and to show all my documents once again. Then I was told to open my panniers and remove the contents.

On this tour, as on most of them, I had stored packets of tea and instant coffee among my luggage as presents for my friends. Once the guards had inspected these, and my socks, and my spare clutch plates and spark plugs, back it all went into the panniers.

I was then ordered to move the bike a few yards to another spot. I waited there for half an hour, during which time they simply stared at me from behind the window of their hut. The barrier remained down. Then I was ordered to move another few yards, followed by more staring and silence.

I thought about this, and the answer dawned on me. So I re-opened one pannier, sorted out two packets of tea and coffee and placed them on the bike's seat. I waited for five minutes, then moved a few yards away from the bike. Out from their hut came the guards, and with the speed of a striking serpent, the tea and coffee disappeared under their coats. They sauntered back to the hut and up went the barrier.

This open bribery was also done with badges and stickers at various times. One just had to judge the situation on the spot and hope one was not offering a bribe to a dyed-in-the-wool guard who was being difficult because he saw me as an enemy, rather than in the hope of being offered something. This would have been fatal.
I never blamed them for this. They system was really the cause of it all, and as I have said, some guards and policemen were most embarrassed and apologetic at the work they had to do.

Conversely, there was the reaction of a border guard to the sight of the AJS, which I was riding on that occasion. It was on the border between East and West Germany. Having progressed through all the passport and visa checks, I was stopped at the final barrier where the unsmiling guard demanded ten Marks for 'permission to drive on East German roads'. Of course, no such permission was needed and what he was really demanding was some pocket money.

I refused to pay, we he argued about it for several minutes while I stood shaking my head, eventually raising his voice to a pitch which alerted his partner, who came running out of the office to see what the fuss was about. As soon as he saw my bike he threw his arms in the air, embraced me and then fumbled in his jacket pocket. He produced a photo of himself astride a 1937 AJS.

The first guard told him I was refusing to hand over any money, but he was brushed aside. 'AJS good, AJS good,' he kept saying to me. Then he said 'No fine' and raised the barrier, so on that occasion I got away without having to sink to bribery. So often did the bike prove to be the ambassador.

Chapter Eleven
CZECHOSLOVAKIA 1974

In 1974 I was again heading across France, Belgium and Germany to the border at Rozvadov. This time I got the impression that the Czech border guards were particularly nervous. There was much menacing with sub-machine guns and they were even more indifferent than usual about offering information or help.

The roads in Czechoslovakia varied widely then, from very good to appalling. Signposting was either not easy to see or non-existent. On most of the tighter bends there was the dreaded pavé, or cobbles. The name makes no difference, but rain on them certainly does.

I learned to live with pavé, but the other fiendish bike destroyers were the many railway level crossings. Did I say level? If ever there was a contradiction in terms this was it. They could be negotiated only at a walking pace.

There was one other hazard and a very intimidating one: giant eight-wheeled armoured personal carriers, taking up almost all of the road and always driven at high speed. They were usually in convoys of a dozen or more, and often by the time the last one had passed I had run out of prayers.

One time I was riding behind a venerable Skoda at a sedate pace. The car was suddenly flung down what was quite a steep bank in what might have been a suicide attempt. Then, coming straight at me, was one of these armoured cars. Whether Czech or Russian, they seemed to enjoy passing as close as they could to oncoming traffic.

Between Plzen and Horovice, road crews were starting to prepare the ground for the motorway that was being built westwards from Prague. Thus the old road became more hazardous, with great earthmoving vehicles cavorting all over the place, often depositing some of their load on the road. I was to observe the progress of this motorway for the next fifteen years, often being switched on to diabolical surfaces when the works demanded it.

If by now you are wondering why I even bothered to put myself through all this when I was supposed to be on holiday, let me tell you of the six questions very seriously asked of me when crossing into Czechoslovakia from Germany. The questions never varied and neither did the sequence. I could have won money by betting a travelling companion that I would be asked: Have you a radio? Have you a calculator? Have you binoculars? Have you any Western Newspapers? have you a Camera? Have you a Bible? (This last one was particularly serious.)

The East Germany border list was similar, with the exception that the first question was whether I had a pistol and ammunition! Perhaps I looked like a one-man Army.

But on to Prague, and meeting Frank and his family again before heading south-east for Gottwaldov and the Four-Stroke Rally campsite. This turned out to be as marvellous as the first, well organised by Vaclav and his wife Jarka, who did much in later years to make it a success. There was much talk and ride-outs with another good mix of European nationalities before the ritual of good-byes. Promising to visit again the following year, I kicked my Matchless into life and rode out of the camp to much waving, and no doubt to mixed feelings from my East European friends. I was free to go.

Riding home, I took a few risks by taking minor roads sometimes in order to see a little more of the country. It was important to pick my moment in doing this, because the authorities took a dim view of any alien straying from the main routes across the country.

I mentioned the two brothers' troubles after stopping in a military zone. This was another point to be borne in mind. Merely pulling over to look at your map could land you in big trouble, and taking out a camera would have been still worse. However, the whole point about these military zones is that they were secret. There were rarely any indications that a traveller was entering or leaving one, and certainly no signposts. Maybe I suffered a slight attack of insensitivity, but about ten miles south of the Polish border I fell foul of the military. It was mildly upsetting at the time.

Meandering along a fairly wild piece of road between tall pine trees, I suddenly came upon a great gathering of Russian armour. The road ahead was blocked by some menacing-looking soldiers. I stopped as quickly as possible and was soon surrounded by many Oriental-looking soldiers. After a painful prod from a sub-machine gun I was virtually lifted off the bike.

An officer appeared and snapped some orders. I was marched into an empty hut and the door was slammed behind me. My immediate worry was for my bike and luggage, but here was nothing I could do. It was pitch black inside the hut, and only after getting used to the dark could I see my watch. I noted the time. Two hours passed before the door was opened and I was marched off to another hut, prodded along by two very keen young soldiers.

The officer who had ordered my incarceration was seated at a table. To my surprise, he spoke to me in good English. He asked why I was on this road, where I came from and where I was going. I had an answer ready. I explained that I had unfortunately misread my map and apologised for having left the main route. He was very understanding, and I came to learn over the next few years that most Russian officers really were gentlemen.

My worries over the Matchless proved to be unfounded. I was led to an open tent where a soldier had parked it carefully on its stand. Its load appeared untouched and my helmet and gloves were on the seat. You can go, they said, and I did, but not before giving the officer a handful of rally badges and stickers.

It was during difficult moments like this that I would recall my wife's words. Just before I left home on these jaunts, Lil would habitually tell me that I would end up in Siberia one day.

Chapter Twelve
CZECHOSLOVAKIA 1975
DAVE GILBERT

Despite Lil's fears about the salt mines, we decided that we would both go to the 1975 Four-Stroke Rally and use my 1970 BSA 650 Thunderbolt and Palma sidecar. Dave Gilbert, a friend from London and an enthusiastic motorcycle tourist, had also promised to attend. We agreed to meet there.

I took as many spares as I thought I could get away with, in the event of my luggage being searched at a border. This required a little subterfuge, since I might be riding a Matchless and carrying spares for, say, Ariel and Norton machines. It was the only way my Czech friends could get them, circumstances being very different from those in Western Europe.

In fact, keeping their bikes on the road at all often necessitated quite remarkable ingenuity. Parts would be grafted on from a variety of sources, engines and frames and wheels and petrol tanks would be cannibalised, nothing would be wasted. I mentioned that Frank Svata had an Ariel 350, and so he did. But it was an Ariel with a front end from a Czech CZ and various other modified or homemade parts.

Using the sidecar outfit this time meant we could carry more spares than usual, and it was a heavily loaded BSA and Palma that headed for Ramsgate. I took my usual route to Rozvadov. It was a hot, muggy day to begin with. This later deteriorated into the grandfather of all thunderstorms, washing out our notions of camping, so we popped into a hotel a few miles from the Czech border.

The next day we set off in glorious sunshine. As we neared the border I kept glancing at Lil in the sidecar, trying to read her thoughts as she saw the various military signboards warning Western armies that they were nearing the Eastern Bloc.

She seemed untroubled by our leaving Germany, and I think she assumed that that was that. Then we rode up to the Communist border barriers and I saw her grow apprehensive. As she saw the armed guards I reminded her: do nothing, say nothing. Leave it to me. She did just that, watching and no doubt wondering why nobody seemed to want to help.

An hour and a half later we were through and riding along the now familiar road to Plzen and on to Prague. Lil was much happier by now, and more so still as we received another wonderful welcome from Frank and Jana. At last they had met Lil.

We had been searched a bit more thoroughly than usual at the border, probably because of the extra capacity of the outfit over a solo, but as usual I had made very sure I could answer 'No' truthfully to the customary six questions. But on every visit I took some practical domestic item to give as a present. They sound like very humble gifts when I say that they were things like an electric iron or a little food mixer, but such everyday items were almost unobtainable there. Or, if they could be found, they were of the poorest quality.

There was one way to buy decent quality goods, and that was to use Western currency in one of the State-run shops. However, that was out of the question for the average citizen. Prices there were high even by Western standards. I remember visiting the Tuzec shop in Prague and noticing that a bottle of Scotch Whisky was priced at about three times what I would pay for it at home, and a tin of instant coffee more like ten times as much.

There was another purpose to the shops, beyond attracting hard currency. They were found only in the larger towns and cities like Prague, Brno and Bratislava. These were the places most commonly visited by tourists, and having window displays of quality goods helped to create a false impression of prosperity.

We had two marvellous days with Frank and Jana and their sons Tomas and Daniel, then left them on the northern road route to Brno, Gottwaldov, Uherske Hradiste, Vsetin and on to the auto campsite at Hovezi, nearly two hundred miles to the east of Prague. Here we had another wonderful reception from our Eastern European friends and those from the West. David Gilbert was there with a friend, their plan being to enjoy the rally and then travel on to Lublin in Poland for the FIM Rally.

But things went tragically wrong for Dave, although to begin with we all enjoyed an interesting serious of runs and meetings at the camp. It was harrowing for everyone there, made still worse because it was the first time I had taken Lil behind the Iron Curtain.

We had left the campsite early one morning for a trip into the Tatra Mountains, and arranged a visit to the Tatra vehicle museum high up in the lovely spot. The run and the tour were marvellous, but it was here, gathered in the canteen for some refreshment, that I was maybe given a clue to the cause of later events. Dave mentioned that when his BMW was under load it was misfiring slightly. I suggested it could be the spark plugs breaking down, perhaps because of the poor Czech petrol, and he planned to fit new ones when he got back to camp.

Now, because mine was the only outfit in the party of about forty riders, my sidecar was used to store everybody's helmets, gloves and other gear, to save them having to carry them around all the time. This meant that I had to wait until last before Lil could climb into the sidecar and we could set off back to the camp.

Just as I started the Thunderbolt, Vaclav walked over and told me that on one of the Czech riders was having problems with his bike. It was a Matchless G80, just like the one back in my garage in Devon, so I switched off again and went to have a look. We dismantled it in the car park and found that the clutch centre boss had stripped its splines. This was quite a blow, but another Czech rider said he had a friend who might have a spare. This friend lived only a few miles away so he rode off to call on him, returning after an hour or so with the exact part we needed. This was nothing short of a miracle, given the dire shortage of spares in Czechoslovakia. You might think that this anonymous friend's generosity was therefore another miracle, but my travels have shown me again and again that it is the people who have almost nothing who are usually the most generous of all.

We fixed the clutch, screwing the primary chaincase on firmly to compensate for the damaged gasket. This would get its rider home, and he could fit a new gasket in his workshop.

Lil and I therefore arrived back at the campsite long after everyone else, and as the outfit swung through the gate we were met by a very serious-faced Swedish friend. Thank God you have come, he said. Your friend Dave has had a bad accident.

Dave had crashed only a few yards from the campsite entrance, but not while riding back from the Tatra trip. He had made it back safely from that run, then changed his plugs as he had earlier discussed with me. He had written some postcards, then went off to post them and to give the engine a trial run at the same time. Riding back towards camp, he had collided with an oncoming Moskvich car at a slight bend in the road.

This had happened only half an hour before Lil and I returned, and the smashed bike and car had not been moved since the accident. I went to look, sickening as the sight was. It was obvious that the car was in its correct position on the road, but now minus a front wing and door, both on the offside, and its windscreen. The BMW was a good thirty yards further on, lying on its side on the grass verge. Its nearside cylinder barrel and crashbar had been smashed off, and there was further damage resulting from its sliding down the road.

I later found out that Dave has been projected forward at such a rate that he had knocked out the car's windscreen and then catapulted up the road. He had also lost his left arm in the accident. An ambulance had arrived, and a passing motorist who had stopped had picked up the severed arm for the ambulance crew. Dave had been rushed to Vsetin, a small town about fifteen miles away. The policeman guarding the wreckage told me that he did not think Dave would live, and that very soon the secret police would arrive to question us.

So, in spite of my feelings, I had to hurry back to his tent and search his belongings for anything that might be at all awkward or incriminating in the eyes of a secret policeman.

I found his visa. It was marked: 'Reason for visit: to attend a motorcycle rally', so I burned it and hoped for the best. I could find nothing else.

The detectives arrived and I was closely questioned for two hours. They repeatedly asked to see Dave's visa, and I said that I assumed he had been carrying it when he crashed, in which case his clothes at the hospital should be searched. (I knew they would be searched in any case). They finally seemed to accept this reasoning. Every word I said was taken down on a typewriter, and I was told that I must get Dave's motorcycle out of the country at once. It was at this time that I also received the news that he was dead.

They left, telling me that they would be back the following day and that I was to make myself available when they arrived.

I shall never forget the effect of all this on the entire camp. All of a sudden, none of the rallyists seemed to have anything to say. We held a meeting late that night which was amongst the saddest I have ever attended. We agreed to carry on with a much-reduced programme of events, and of course we had to arrange transport to get the battered BMW to the West German border. I also had to call the British Embassy in Prague and explain everything, and they promised to inform Dave's parents in London.

Early the next morning the police returned and the grilling resumed. This time they were quite abrupt and ordered me to get things moving immediately. We borrowed a lorry and took the BMW to Vsetin railway station, where a helpful railwayman gave us a large crate. We dismantled the bike into three large pieces, crated it up and asked to pay for carriage to London. Then the blow was delivered: that wasn't possible under present law, as from Vsetin it could be sent only as far as the West German border.

So I telephoned Bill Slocombe, the dealer in London from whom Dave had bought the bike. I explained everything and Bill immediately agreed to telegraph the money for the rest of the journey to the border railway station. He was enormously helpful and I was very grateful to him, for he helped me out of a difficult spot.

The day after Dave's death, every single rallyist walked from the camp along the road to the spot where he crashed. We held a little private service and flowers were placed beside a small wooden cross on the grass verge where Dave had lain. It was a very sad and solemn occasion, and grief shared by such a family of nations was humbling and beautiful.

Over the following days I reflected for many hours, looking at the accident from many angles, studying the road and remembering the weather conditions. As Dave was an experienced and sensible motorcyclist, I came down to three possible causes of his accident. Having changed his plugs, he may not have solved the misfiring and may have glanced down at the engine. The tendency is always to drift to one side when doing this. Or the low, setting sun may have just caught him on the slight curve in the road. Or he could have momentarily forgotten which side of the road he should have been on.

I decided it must have been the first possibility. I reckoned I knew him well enough to discount the other two. What a blessing he did not have his friend on the pillion when he crashed.

Lil and I left Hovezi in a subdued mood. With a final phone call to the British Embassy in Prague, I learned that Dave's body was to be flown to London for burial in Forest Hill in East London, his home. Our outfit was loaded down with his riding and camping kit. His friend and passenger had decided to continue on to the FIM Rally in Poland, and had arranged a ride with another rider.

We had a few days in and around Prague trying to forget the previous week. Frank and Jana did their best to help, and took us out to see something we might otherwise have missed. Frank took us to Kamen, Statni Hrad, and here was a wonderful sight: the national motor museum. Housing Jawa and CZ motorcycles from the first days of the Padget-designed bikes up to the latest from the factories. There was also Stasny's racing bike that Bill Ivy had ridden.

The time came to leave for home. I am always sad to leave Prague. It is a beautiful city, and leaving such dear friends behind makes the leaving sadder still.

We arrived at the border at Rozvadov ready for the usual delays. This time things were different. The swaggering, unsmiling border guard checked our papers and gleefully announced that we had not had our visa stamped at Hovezi. I realised that he was right. I knew very well that at every campsite, I had to get the controller to make my visa and add the length of my stay. But in the aftermath of Dave's death I had forgotten to get this done, and now I had made this border guard's day. He told me that he was fining me two hundred crowns.

Poor Lil was quite distressed, but with a rather forced display of confidence I told her not to worry. I would go to the bank there at the border post, change some money and be back in a few minutes.

I was marched over to change sterling for crowns. After much rigmarole I bought two hundred crowns for ten pounds, walked back to the guard standing by my bike and handed it over. Without a word, he turned on his heel and went off into his hut. We waited.

He soon reappeared, accompanied by a Russian officer who ordered him to give me back my money. The Russian and I looked at each other, and to my astonishment I realised that it was the officer who'd questioned me on my previous trip east when I had chanced upon the Red Army on manoeuvres! 'Englishman will not pay fine,' he said. 'Pardon - you must go back to *Banka*.'

Here there was a slight snag. It was not possible to buy sterling with crowns as regulations did not permit it. However, I could buy Swedish kroner with my crowns, so I did that. I was going to Sweden the following year anyway. Ironically, in the end I worked out that I gained about ten pence on the deal with the various exchange rates. Lil was both relieved and incredulous over the outcome. I had not told her about my two-hour imprisonment in the hut so I couldn't very well explain why a Russian Officer should do me a favour, so I just said that I had friends in the Kremlin!

Many thunderstorms later we were in Calais and soon making tracks across southern England, the BSA going as well as ever. Of course, my sad job to follow was to visit Dave's parents. It was a miserable journey, and unfortunately, owing to many reasons, Dave's body arrived home and was buried before I even knew, so I was unable to be there. Such was usually the complexity of dealing with the Eastern Bloc.

Scotland Tour 1948

Portland
Matchless 350cc
1948

Scotland
Matchless
1949

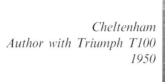

Cheltenham
Author with Triumph T100
1950

1

Ireland
Author with Matchless
1951

Jawa 500 OHC
(never imported to G.B.)
1951

Dover
July 1952

Calais
July 1952

French Alps
Matchless 350
1952

Isle of Man
Author's wife, Lil with G80
1967

Isle of Man
Author's wife, Lil with G80
1967

*Isle of Man
Author
1967*

*Prague
Soviet Tank
1974*

*Stary Hrozenkov
Dave Pope & Vaclav
1974*

4

Stary Hrozenkov
Dave Pope and an array of
Norton and Matchless
1974

Czechoslavakia
Vaclav
1974

Czechoslavakia
Author receives
trophy
1974

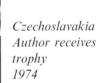

5

Dave Gilbert Funeral 1976

*Hovezi
Czechoslavakia
Bob, Vaclav,
Author, Joseph.
1977*

Plumlov
Czechoslavakia
Author about to ride
in competition
1979

Czechoslavakia
Author, Bob,(Eng)
Vaclav, Jarka,(CZ)
Rolf, (Sweden)
1979

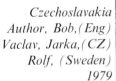

Morlaix, France
Hervé with AJS
Terrot S/C
1985

7

Visa to enter East Germany (Check Point Charlie) and cross the country within 24 hours, and enter Poland.

Berlin's glasnost rally

THE Berlin Wall has been well and truly buried — for the first time ever, East Germany's bikers are able to organise a rally with their Western comrades.

The Motorsportelus Post Berlin (East) and the Classic British Bike Club of West Berlin are to meet on Communist soil in May.

"We hope this will be the first of many get-togethers," said Devon-based Dick Powell of the BMF. "At last a dream has been realised."

For more information about the rally, which takes place from May 25-27, write to: Gunter Niese, Josef Nawrocki, Str 13, Berlin 1162, DDR.

FIM go Yugo for summer knnes-up

THIS year's FIM rally takes place in Belgrade, capital of Yugoslavia. Entry fee is 200 Swiss Francs (about £80). It's a four-day rally from June 20-24. Entry forms from the BMF, 129 Seaforth Avenue, Motspur Park, New Malden, Surrey KT3 6UJ.
Camping is available and should be paid for along with the entry.

A comment on the "Rally to Come" and future F.I.M. Rally

Stary Hrozenkov Four Stroke Rally Post Card

Norway AJS at Arctic Circle 1995

Chapter Thirteen
CZECHOSLOVAKIA 1976

In 1976 my European journey was again to be to Czechoslovakia, but this time I would be travelling alone. Lil could not bring herself to go again after the previous year's disaster.

My destination was Hovezi as usual, via Prague. When receiving my invitation from Vaclav, I was touched to see that I would not be attending the Four-Stroke Rally but the Dave Gilbert Memorial Rally. I took the hovercraft from Ramsgate as usual and left Calais in exceptionally hot weather. Violent thunderstorms overtook me as I reached Germany and battled down the E5 motorway.

Anyone who has travelled in wet weather on the heavy, fast traffic on German motorways will know that it is a battle. It is a struggle to see or be seen, the water forms ponds much more than it does on British motorways, and the spray from vehicles overtaking me at around twice my speed creates and extra hazard. It turned out to be my wettest ride ever through Germany.

Again I negotiated the challenge of the border crossing, and the G80 and I headed for Prague. It was beginning to seem like a home city to me; I was always fascinated by its character and old-world charm. By way of contrast I could never forget the condition of many of the city's roads with their huge potholes, cobbles and tramlines everywhere.

In fact the tramlines were a double hazard, being set with a large gap between the line and the cobbled street surface. This was quite wide enough to accept a motorcycle's front wheel. It sounds like a cue for the old joke about having to ride to the tram terminus to get the wheels out of the rut, but it didn't seem that funny at the time.

Settled down in Frank and Jana's sitting room after dinner that evening, I noticed that as usual, they did not draw the curtains. As they looked out on other windows at the same height across the road, I asked why this was. This was a real insight into the more sinister aspects of life in a beautiful city. 'Many eyes will be watching,' Frank acknowledged, but he deliberately let them see so as to avoid a raid or other intrusion. Once he had said it, I could practically feel the binoculars trained on me and someone reading my lips.

With the subject opened up, Frank also told me about the Lenin poster in the hallway. 'It's for my visitor the day after you leave,' he said. It was a fact that after I left for home each year, a secret policeman came to their flat and questioned Frank about me and the reasons for my visit.

The sinister theme continued the next morning. Frank had to go to work and I decided to walk about Prague, do some sight-seeing and maybe a little shopping. As I left the building and entered the sunny street I saw two young men looking in a shop window on the other side of the road. I walked along for a minute or two, then spun round and saw the same men not far behind me. They immediately become engrossed in another window display. I walked on, then angled myself while

70

looking in a window so as to see their reflections. Without doubt, they were following me.

I carried on, deciding to make them work for their living. I turned right and left, stopping here and there, until I entered a department store. Here I had great fun moving from counter to counter, walking back the way I had come and passing by them, then walking back the way I had come and passing by them, then walking back the same way again. Each time they adjusted their position to keep me in view.

Then came my masterstroke. I got on to a crowded escalator. As it reached the next floor I managed to slip off and get straight on to another one going down. I crouched down amongst my fellow travellers and got clean away. James Bond had nothing on me that day! For the rest of my spree in Prague I was untroubled and felt quite jubilant. Frank did not seem unduly worried over the incident when I told them about it that evening.

The next day I left and rode through Brno and Gottwaldov, finally reaching the campsite. It was another great gathering, in quality if not in numbers. I was pleased to see a friend from England, Bob Bartholomew, with three other Velocette club members.

Whenever riders gather there is always talk. This was always so interesting at these Czech rallies, having mind to the many nationalities represented. Language is never a complete barrier, and even the misunderstandings can help things along. Bob was asked to use a typical British toast when about to tip down a drink. A rallyist from every other nation had used his country's normal toasting expression. Bob rose from his seat, somewhat wobbly due to the effects of several rounds of slivovitz, thought hard and came out with 'Here's mud in your eye' before heading for the toilets.

This left me to explain to all the Europeans and Scandinavians just what the hell it meant. I've never understood it myself, so instead I led a chorus of 'Mud in your eye' before following Bob.

We held a service in memory of Dave Gilbert. The whole company rode to the church at Hovezi. To our amazement and gratitude, we saw that the local club had fashioned and placed in position a large flat stone with two BMW cylinder barrels set either side of a raised stone tablet, with a suitable inscription in English. This was most touching. Vaclav and his friends gave me some flowers to lay upon it and the whole group shared the solemn occasion. We then rode back to the spot where Dave had crashed, where more fresh flowers were already in place in a jar by the side of the road.

As a further mark of respect, the rally badge that we always received during these events was now inscribed DGMR. What great fellows our Czech hosts were.

After the rally was over and everyone had left, I stayed with Vaclav and his family for a few days at their home in Gottwaldov. Jarka, Vaclav's wife, asked me if I would like to help her do the shopping. I thought this would be a good chance to see something of the town and to compare its shops with those in the bigger towns and cities.

Now I must explain that at that time there were many Cuban students in Gottwaldov. I think that they were part of a student exchange scheme, and I was told that they had priority on buses, in any public place and in the shops. Jarka and I were waiting in a queue at a meat counter. Meat was always in short supply in Czechoslovakia, and as we gradually moved along we could see the cuts for sale diminishing. As we reached the front of the queue there was one joint left.

72

Behind us all the while in the queue were three Cuban boys chattering in Spanish. When they realised that there was only one good piece of meat left, they stepped in front of us and made to buy it. Now I am not normally given to argument or to making a fuss in public, but this really annoyed me. I pushed them all out of the way and insisted that it be sold to Jarka. It seemed to take them completely by surprise. They said nothing, the startled shopkeeper handed it over, Jarka paid and we left.

As soon as I had done it I wondered if I had done wrong. Would it be remembered, and would Jarka and her family suffer because of it after I had left? But she didn't seem worried, and in fact was happy that we had the makings of dinner that night.

Leaving the Hamsiks, I headed the G80 north to Prerov, then northwest to Ostrava, a very pleasant large town near the Polish border. Here I met a rare tourist, a Russian motorcyclist on their much-coveted M72, the Soviet copy of the BMW. My Russian is practically non-existent, but he knew some German and Czech so we managed to have a chat of sorts by sticking to mechanical talk on motorcycling. He seemed nervous at first that he should be talking to me, continually glancing in all directions until I suggested we could ride off the road into a clearing in the woods.

Here he settled down a bit. We talked some more and I gave him some stickers and badges and some odd photos I had of motorcycle rallies in Western Europe. As usual, these small gifts produced a reaction that seemed out of all proportion to their value to me. He produced a small lapel badge of the Moscow Motorcycle Club and gave it to me; I still have it. He would not give me his name or address; such was the peculiar world behind the Iron Curtain. So we said goodbye and I rode west.

I still think about that rider from time to time, and the more I do so, the more strange our meeting seems. Who was he, I wonder? Even though we were behind the Iron Curtain, the Soviet Union did not usually allow its citizens as much liberty as that.

It was nearly dark as I reached an autocamp near Hadrec Kralov. The camp controller didn't seem too pleased to see me, but I got the all-important visa stamp. Like most of the auto-camps then, this one had a restaurant serving reasonable food very cheaply, so I was able to eat well and conserve my precious emergency supplies.

My notes remind me that I left at five o'clock the next morning. Keeping to the north of Prague to save time, I arrived at the familiar Rozvodov border control and spent an hour and a half on document inspection and all that goes with it.

At this point it was my usual practice to ride up through Germany and camp for the night at Aachen before the last leg to the French coast, but the weather was so good and I felt so fresh that I kept going. In the end I rode through most of the warm summer night too, arriving at Calais at four in the morning to await the first hovercraft crossing. While doing so I calculated that since leaving the autocamp the previous morning I had covered 875 miles. The Matchless was running faultlessly, returning its usual eighty miles to the gallon.

It was as I was contemplating this that a young couple on a 1000cc BMW rode up beside me. The young lady seemed more interested in the Matchless than the man and was soon telling me that they had a similar 500cc AJS at their home in Suffolk. However, her husband had said that it would not have been up to their recent trip, as they were going to Toulouse and had only one week to do it. When she asked where I had been she became quite excited, calling to her husband to join us. I felt rather awkward as she laid into her loved one, asking why it had been necessary to use their German twin when the AJS could clearly have done it.

I made a mental note to keep my mouth shut but I soon had the couple quite worried again. They asked if I would take a bottle of whisky and one of wine through customs at Ramsgate as it was obvious I had none on my machine. Naturally I agreed, sliding the bottles under the straps holding down my load, but as I rode down the hovercraft ramp and up to the customs I was greeted by an officer who by now had got to know me quite well. He just said 'Czecho again I presume?' grinned and waved me through. I rode around the corner and waited.

The looks on the faces of the BMW couple were a picture as they emerged from the customs shed and into the car park, clearly worried that I was halfway up the A20 with their duty-free booze. Their frowns changed to smiles as the spotted me waving to them.

As we transferred the bottles and talked for a moment or two before separating, it occurred to them that I had made rapid progress through customs. I couldn't resist it, and played them up a bit by saying 'It's the Matchless, you know. Goes further faster.' (This was an old factory slogan.)

Chapter Fourteen
OLD AND NEW AND FAST AND SLOW

'

Why do you ride old stuff like that?' said the rider of the giant machine by which I had stopped. He went on to suggest that my old G80 didn't look much next to his, an 1100cc four-cylinder Yamaha. And he was quite right, for it looked tiny standing next to his.

You don't often come across motorcyclists like this. Many of us are irrational in our choice of machine, but instant criticism of someone else's bike is unusual except between friends. I made some non-committal remark and walked off towards the booking office, but he followed me and started telling me about a G80 he had once owned. It often refused to start, he said, and performance was poor even when it was running.

'Of course,' he said, jerking a thumb at the silver Yamaha, 'I have to have a bike like that.' He didn't enlarge on that statement, but I could see that he wanted me to ask why. But my attention was taken up by the girl at the booking office desk as she dealt with my papers. Then I had to move on to allow my new friend to do the same.

With a few minutes to spare, I looked the Matchless over after the run from Devon and was checking the luggage straps when he returned and restarted our rather one-sided conversation. He commented on the luggage ~I was carrying - in this respect it was my bike that was the giant - and asked why I was taking so much gear on holiday. I replied that it was just a few odd things for friends. 'Looks heavy,' he said, as the sea breeze caused my bike to sway slightly on its prop stand.

His load consisted of one holdall strapped onto the seat behind him, and, bolted to the carrier behind the seat, a glassfibre topbox. As he opened this I saw that it appeared to contain only some rag and a workshop manual. Bearing in mind his previous remarks about his unreliable Matchless, he offered no explanation when he saw me looking at his manual, going on to tell me that he had to travel light as he was going to Belgium. Well, that is no particular reason to travel light at all and I could see that he again wanted me to ask him to explain, but at that moment we were asked to start our bikes and board the hovercraft.

My bike was berthed on one side and the Yamaha on the other. For those not familiarly with the Ramsgate Hovercraft, this meant that he was seated on one side and I was on the other, so our talk was abruptly halted.

I recommend this method of crossing the Channel (which now operates from Dover). The loading staff handle the bikes with great respect and anchor them down with straps, under which they use cushions to prevent the straps rubbing against the paint during the crossing. The other advantage is the time saving, and thirty-five minutes later we were in Calais. Five minutes after that I was on the quay, through French customs and donning helmet and gloves for my day's ride. The Yamaha rider chose to wait a while to check his route, whereas I almost knew mine by heart by this time. I started the bike with a single kick and was away.

I was still thinking about him as I rode steadily out of Calais and along the flat, featureless road to Dunkerque. Rain began to fall and the early morning mist swirled about.

At Dunkerque the G80 was turned into the A25 motorway, heading for Lille. Suddenly there was another rider alongside, not the Yamaha owner, but a young man dressed in a bright orange one-piece waterproof suit and seated on a blue BMW R75. As he drew level he seemed to be studying my bike from front to rear, then raised one hand level with his head to indicate how heavily he thought it was loaded. Then, with a nod and a wave, he sped off and was soon an orange dot on the horizon. I noted from the registration plate that the rider was German too.

I left Lille behind, and Mons and Namur, and then the border crossing at Aachen. At last the rain stopped and some weak sunshine appeared. I carried on at my usual cruising speed of sixty miles an hour. A glance at the speedo reading showed me that I was three hundred miles from Calais - half way, and time for a petrol stop.

Now, for anyone who has never been on a German motorway in midsummer, let me say that they are crowded. Buying petrol can be a slow business in the congested service areas. I tried to turn this to my advantage by giving myself some exercise as I waited, dismounting as I approached the forecourt and pushing my bike to the rear of the queue. I would then push it to a pump, fill up and pay, then push away again. Sitting on a bike for a period of hours can stiffen up the joints.

I rode on past Cologne and Frankfurt, this being the section of the motorway I feared the most. The multiple lanes bypassing Frankfurt are amongst the busiest I have ever seen, used by everything from heavy lorries to very fast cars to dawdling tourists. The lorries often travelled in convoy, causing enough turbulence as they passed me to rock the bike from side to side. As each lorry overtook me the rocking would build up. With a heavy load, it meant taking a real grip of the machine.

There always seemed to be road building going on, too, so traffic was switched from lane to lane. It became almost a competition between drivers as to who could reach the diversion fork first, or at least at the greatest speed.

The weather deteriorated again, the road spray hanging over the surface and the road like a fog. I pressed on, making the best progress I could, as worried about traffic closing on me from behind as by any trouble that might materialise in the spray ahead.

Matchless flexibility comes to the fore in such conditions. Top gear can be held down to a slow pace, yet the bike will respond at once to an opened throttle. The drum brakes were another comforting feature. Things have improved now, but in the 1970s disc brakes on motorcycles were notoriously poor in the wet. A rider would pull the brake lever and next to nothing would happen. He would pull harder and the brake would suddenly grab. I was also always confident that the wettest weather would not cause the Matchless to misfire, whereas modern multi-cylinder machines and even BMW flat twins, with their relatively exposed HT leads, have been known to suffer.

As I neared Nürnberg I stopped again for petrol and more motorcycle pushing exercises when I heard the unmistakable sound of a BMW flat twin behind me. Alongside came my orange-clad friend on his 750. This time he looked me up and down even more and nearly rammed a stationary car. He parked his bike and came across as I filled my tank.

"You go very fast," he said, in a mixture of German and English. "Very, very fast with so much load." "No," I said in my meagre German, "only ninety-five or a hundred kilometres an hour." "No," he insisted. "I saw you at Calais, now you are here and I am here."

Well, there was no disputing that. I looked at him and then looked over at his BMW. I suggested that while he went much faster than I did (and he agreed that he was cruising at a hundred and sixty), so did his petrol. I asked him how many times he had stopped for petrol that day. He pondered on that, then replied that this was his fourth stop.

Yes my friend, I said, you have spent a lot of time at petrol stations today, waiting to buy petrol while I go past. This is my second stop since Calais. So I travel for about an hour and a half longer than you on each tankful of petrol and our average speeds are exactly the same.

As I walked to the kiosk to pay, I said to him, 'You have also spent more Marks than me today.' He agreed ruefully, adding that he was wearing his tyres out faster as well. As I paid he remembered that he still had to fill his own tank, and ran across to his machine as I pushed mine out of the way of the pumps.

I decided to wait for this pleasant young man, and soon he came up on his bike. I snicked my bike into gear and we moved out onto the motorway. Expecting him to accelerate away, I was quite pleased to find that he had settled down behind and slightly to one side of me. We travelled together at my customary speed until reaching the Amberg Junction, where I had to head off east. I indicated my intentions to him, and with a wave he overtook and was soon lost in the maze of traffic as I headed off for the E12.

Eventually, after a long day in the saddle, I reached the familiar camping site at Schnaittenbach at eight o'clock. By now I was less than thirty miles from the Czech border, and after erecting my one-man tent and brewing tea, I sat and gazed at the bike resting on its stand and thought about the German boy on the BMW. What were his thoughts on our encounter?

Then I remembered the Yamaha rider I had met in Kent, and this started me off on another tack again. Why did I continue to use British bikes? Had Japanese bikes been available when I started foreign touring in 1946, and had I bought and ridden them, I just could not have afforded such extensive holidays as I have had. There are two strands to this: the heavy petrol consumption, and the short production run of so many Japanese bikes. Models are introduced and quickly discounted in order to make riders buy new bikes more often.

The other problem with these admittedly sophisticated machines is that much of the maintenance is beyond the scope of the average owner. I estimate that my 2,000 miles services on the G80 (changing the engine oil, cleaning the magneto points, checking chain adjustment and the gearbox and primary case oil levels) take about an hour and cost almost nothing in materials. Importantly, that interval can be stretched while on tour, meaning I can spend more time riding and talking to my friends and even less time with the spanners.

To my mind there was just no substance to the Japanese versus British argument that ran for years in clubrooms and motorcycle magazines. There just was (and is) no argument. One you pay through the nose to ride and enjoy, the other you just ride and enjoy.

This chapter has been more about motorcycles than my holiday that year, but I did continue onto Prague to see my friends. The return journey included a run from Prague to Calais during which I stopped only at borders and for petrol, and by the time I arrived home in Braunton I had covered 4,600 trouble-free miles in fifteen days.

Chapter Fifteen
FINLAND 1977

Just in case you were thinking that all roads lead to Czechoslovakia as far as my bikes are concerned, I should explain that in between my almost ritual annual trips there in the 1970s, Lil and I also made others of a completely different nature.

Winter rallying is a popular pursuit amongst some motorcyclists, and one of the more popular annual rallies is the Elephant, held in Germany. (I have already mentioned the Dragon Rally in Wales.) We attended the Elefantentreffen in 1973 with the BSA and Palma, also towing a trailer loaded mainly with other British rallyists' gear. There were trips to several Dragon Rallies and other club meetings, and in earlier years there were many visits to Ireland, to the Isle of Man for the TT races every June, and to most other points of the British Isles.

But there was one exceptional trip that I made in June 1977. A conflict of loyalties meant deciding between Czechoslovakia and Finland, to visit a very good friend at Turku.

Once again I loaded up the G80. Once more it found itself carrying me across foreign land, this time on unfamiliar roads.

The ferry docked at Göteborg in Sweden and I rode briskly along the excellent road via Jönköping and Linköping to Stockholm, where I caught another ferry to Helsinki. I was carrying no visa and hoping for the best. Using the ferry journey to catch up on some sleep, I landed at Helsinki quite fresh but then had to ride back west to Turku and my friend Enko.

He suggested a trip up to the Russian border. I wanted to see it, and thus far my passport and RAC International driving licence had sufficed. I had no idea exactly what Enko had in mind, but approaching the border the next day my heart was beating fast and I wondered what was going to happen.

The border guards looked at me in amazement, but Enko, whose Russian was as perfect as his English, seemed to convince both the Finnish and the Russian guards that they should let us through. He asked me to show them my RAC document, which I produced with a suitable flourish. I have never understood why it had the effect that it did, but they seemed to take it as truly international and we passed through with much nodding and smiling on both sides.

Travel was heavily restricted in the Soviet Union at that time. Foreigners had to disclose their destination and were permitted to travel a maximum of one hundred and fifty miles a day. They were expected to report to the police at the appropriate place after each day's travel. Yet here we were heading for Leningrad. I could hardly believe it, and deep down I felt very uneasy.

My worries were soon to be justified. We had ridden about fifty miles past the border when two cars overtook us and pulled up in front. Many men jumped out and waved us to a halt. Some were in uniform and some in civilian clothing, but all were very menacing and began to shout and wave their arms about. For the first time, Enko began to look worried.

My passport was examined, and this time the RAC licence did me no good. I was separated from Enko and made to start up the Matchless and follow one of the cars back the way we had come. Enko was escorted towards Leningrad.

At the border I was literally pushed back into Finland. This time there were no smiling faces. I rode back to Turku wondering about Enko. However, on reaching his parents' house I was told that he had phoned them. He said that all was well but that he would be in the Soviet Union for several days, and that I should return to England.

I eventually found out what happened to him. He was interrogated, of course, but he coped well. He said I was just someone who had happened to arrive at the border post at the same time as him and had happened to be waved through at the same time. Possibly the border guards were so embarrassed that they also made up some story or other. What a pity they did not stamp my passport!

There was a strange echo of this incident some years later, in 1986. The huge annual FIM Rally was being staged that year in Budapest. (It was just about the best FIM rally I have ever attended, but that's another story.) I had arrived at the Hungarian border and came upon several other British riders. Queuing to get through border control, I heard someone shouting my name. One of the guards came up, and then I remembered him from a previous trip. I had given him some badges and stickers, and some advice on his old Norton ES2.

'Come.' He said, ushering me through a side door as you might say. He grabbed my passport, reappeared moments later, and I shoved it in my pocket. A few more words of thanks and I was on my way.

But on leaving the rally and heading north for Czechoslovakia, I came unstuck at the border. 'You are very bad,' the guard said, and showed me my open passport. To my horror I saw that there was no entry stamp in it. My mind flashed back to my special treatment on entering the country. Not much help after all, I thought.

I was kept in the control room and told that I had a choice. I could go to jail overnight, or I could ride back to my point of entry. I didn't like the sound of either. I protested that it was the fault of the border guard. That didn't work, and I hadn't expected it to.

Then I had an idea and decided it was s worth trying. Marching boldly up to the desk, I slammed down my RAC international driving licence. I thumped the table again, pointed to it and said 'International' very slowly and meaningfully. To my surprise, the effect was immediate. 'International,' they repeated to each other, then gave me back all my documentation and let me pass.

Heading for Bratislava, I wanted to laugh out loud in spite of my friend's administrative bungle. The power of a single word! The RAC would have been pleased to see it, I'm sure.

Chapter Sixteen
CZECHOSLOVAKIA 1977

Following the Finnish adventure, that year's trip to the Four-Stroke Rally seemed easy in comparison. It was held at Stity, near the Polish border, at a lovely wooded campsite. For a change I decided to use my 1973 Triumph Tiger 750, a twin-cylinder machine which I had bought new.

I travelled alone but met up again with Bob Bartholomew. By this time I had also made many friends amongst the Swedish riders who were equally dedicated visitors to this rally. We were always made to feel that simply by taking the trouble to visit, we were giving them hope for the future and providing that they were not forgotten.

I was standing in a queue outside the rally control building with Rolf, a Swedish friend and sidecar-cross fanatic. He would race either as a driver or passenger; he didn't mind. We were joined by a large group of boisterous Eastern Bloc riders. A few moments later an officious gentleman climbed on to a pair of steps near the door and, with accompanying arm-waving, shouted 'All comrades this side, all capitalists this side!'

I felt quite pleased; a capitalist at last! Strangely enough, nobody seemed upset by this and we obediently formed up as instructed.

Riding away from Stity after the rally, I remembered that I had some postcards to send. I found a post-box, surrounded by a group of Russian soldiers. I had to force my way through before I cold drop my cards into the gaping hole one always found on post-boxes in this part of the world. None of them ever reached England; no doubt they had been retrieved by the Russians and kept as souvenirs.

Chapter Seventeen
MORE LOCAL CUSTOMS

As I have mentioned, on my trips to Eastern Europe, I would always take as many spare parts for my friends as I could possibly carry - the limitations being my bike's carrying capacity and border guards' credulity. Nortons and Matchlesses had been exported to Czechoslovakia until about 1965, but spares sources in the country had long since dried up. I also used to take Western motorcycle badges, stickers, literature on bikes, and indeed any other magazines that I thought I would be able to get past border controls. This was all a matter of experience, and as the years went by I grew bolder.

The shortages of the most ordinary items could be so ridiculous as to be almost funny. In Prague, the plastic carrier bag was a prized rarity. During my 1974 trip, my host Frank introduced me to some friends at their south Bohemia home. I gave them a plastic bag containing a few things. The bag itself bore the logo of the British Motorcyclists Federation.

Some time later, back in Prague and walking along the main shopping street of Vaclav Nemesti, I realised I was walking behind a young girl who was swinging a BMF carrier bag to and fro as she walked. She received many envious glances from passers-by. Was it the one I had brought? There can't have been many in the country!

I did not always take my camera with me. This would seem an obvious mistake, and I do wish I had better photographic record of my trips east, but its use was always severely restricted by the military and the secret police. Then again, I could not record everything with a picture, for who would believe me? Who would have believed that a city square in Prague had been re-named, in 1969, Soviet Tanske Square? At least I managed to photograph the accursed tank on its plinth.

Who at home would have believed the size and the number of billboards at every vantagepoint, selling not consumer goods but political dogma? Or how, out in the smaller towns and villages, there were loudspeakers in the trees blaring out propaganda to intimidate the people? Or how, whenever a Czech flag was flown, there always had to be two Red Flags with it, one on either side. Each Eastern Bloc country had its own version of all this, but the meaning was always the same.

Chapter Eighteen
HONDAS, HARLEYS AND BORDER GUARDS

I had been with Frank and his family once again. This time, another friend from Prague invited me to travel with him to a meeting in Duba.

When the time came to leave, he pulled up on a Honda 250. This I could hardly believe, but the explanation was straight-forward enough. The Honda had been bought by the Jawa works for study and evaluation. My friend worked in the plating department there, and had somehow managed to buy the bike when Jawa had finished with it. It was probably the only Honda in the Czech capital at that time.

We motored steadily towards Duba, which is north of Prague, and as we came in sight of the autocamp in the valley below us, we stopped to admire the view. We were being looked at too, for as we remounted and rolled down the road and reached the entrance, we were immediately surrounded by dozens of riders greeting us with handshakes, slaps on the back and general enthusiasm. I recognised many Continental friends, including Gunter from East Berlin, whom I had not expected to see that year.

One person was not pleased to see us. He marched up to me just as I was finally able to get off the Matchless, and in poor English he demanded to know why I had not reported to him first. This did not surprise me, as by now I was well conditioned to life behind the Curtain, so I adopted a suitably humble demeanour and went with him to his office.

Once inside, his attitude changed completely. He shook my hand and asked, 'How come you know so many riders? You are English, are you not?' speaking carefully, I replied that I had visited the country before and had sometimes noticed other riders. Motorcyclists were generally friendly to each other, and so we had sometimes talked. So yes, I knew a few of the riders there.

It sounded weak, even to me, but I did not want to tell him that I had met many of the riders outside his door at the Four-Stroke Rally, for the reasons I have mentioned earlier. At this stage I did not know who this man was, or his intentions. But I did now understand why this rally appeared so open. His very presence - camp controller, secret policeman or whatever he was - meant that the event had the approval of the State.

There were some interesting bikes there, including some really ingenious specials. Motorcyclists the world over have been constructing specials for decades, putting one manufacturer's engine into another's frame, then uprating the brakes or the suspension, or indeed making their own parts. Usually it is done to improve performance; to make a better bike, at least in the eyes of the owners. Here it was done in order to keep a bike on the road, and some of the mixtures of British and Continental bikes were remarkable pieces or work. The Honda was barely visible all weekend under a crowd of interested riders.

Leaving Duba in the company of Czech friends, there was another surprise. Soon after striking camp we came across a large group of Harley-Davidsons on the road. We followed them for a while until they turned off into another campsite. After a few minutes' deliberation, we went in too. I was curious to know how so many Harleys came to be there. It was more or less an official event, according to the friendly Czech organiser, although there were no British riders there. Most were German, Austrian and Czech, but there was one Canadian. I would have like to have met him, but we had to press on.

Two days later, after an early start from Frank's flat, I rode off to my favourite border crossing at Rozvodov. It was raining, and Czech roads can be slightly disturbing in the wet, but I was there before nine o'clock and quickly through the first barrier.

I pulled up behind a French-registered car, in which sat a man and his wife and two little girls. I could see immediately that he was an inexperienced traveller in this part of the world, for he remained seated in his car. This was almost always taken by a border guard as indicating a lack of respect. Well, I could do nothing about it so I sat on the G80 waiting to see what would happen. The rain was pouring down by this time, and the only shelter was the canopy under which two guards were standing.

Suddenly, both of them walked briskly up to the car, ripped open the doors and virtually dragged out the driver and his wife. The doors were slammed shut, whereupon their daughters started screaming and beating the windows. This became too much for the guards. They opened the doors again and out rushed the children. This was disturbing enough, but now followed a scene which took some taking.

The bigger of the guards had pinned the Frenchman against a wall by pushing the barrel of his sub-machine gun against his throat. They kept his wife and children apart, by the table set out in front of the control building. They brought every suitcase out of the car and emptied the contents on to the table, which was wet from the rain blowing under the shelter. Everything was sifted through, including all the lady's personal things, and only after the last bag from the car had been checked did they release the husband. He was furious by this time, and they then had to gather their wet belongings together and try to re-pack.

Then one of the guards spotted the lady's bag, hanging from her shoulder on a strap. He grabbed it and emptied that on to the table as well, the contents spilling over the road. This brought a cry of rage from the man, who tried to grab it and was rewarded by being marched back to the wall at gunpoint.

Then came the most despicable thing I had seen for a long time. The two little girls were carrying small decorated purses. These too were snatched away. The children screamed in fright, and at that moment I quite involuntarily decided that was enough and started walking towards them. I really don't know what I would have done had I reached the guards, but then a gun was swung round and aimed at me, so I just froze. The purses were emptied on to the table as well.

My heart went out to that French family. Then, as suddenly as this brutality had started, it stopped. They moved their car off to one side and disappeared into the control building. Fortunately for me, the guards also disappeared and two much older ones dealt with me. I didn't see that family again, and passed into Germany feeling sad and angry at the same time.

I remember another odd incident with a Czech policeman just east of Brno. My route had taken me through some lovely country, the roads were clear of traffic and I was really enjoying myself. Then a Jawa went past me and the policeman on it waved me down.

He dismounted and walked up to me, then circled the bike noting the GB plate, motioned for me to remain seated on the Matchless, went back to his bike and withdrew a large book from one of its panniers. It took at least twenty minutes for him to find the page he was looking for, whereupon he walked back to me and pushed the opened book under my nose. He pointed to a sentence that read 'You are fined 100 crowns for overtaking on a bend.'

I looked behind me at the half-mile straight I had just ridden along. I thought for a bit, but could not remember overtaking anything for at least an hour. But I knew the rules of the game. I paid up; he smiled at last, gave me some meaningless tickets, pocketed the money and beckoned me to continue on my way.

Chapter Nineteen
CZECHOSLOVAKIA 1978

The 1978 Four-Stroke Rally was another great success, during which a revealing episode took place. This time it was held at Plumlov, an autocamp in a lovely wooded area in the centre of the country, near the town of Prostejov.

I arrived there one afternoon after a short stay in Prague. I was greeted by a Swedish friend who told me about a mysterious carload of men who had visited the camp earlier, looked around and then driven off at great speed. I suggested that this was not so very surprising, and had soon put it out of my mind as I mingled with the international family of rallyists.

The next morning, I had just finished a breakfast of cornflakes and tinned milk and was making tea when I heard several cars pulling into the campsite. I was camped on the edge of the site, partly hidden from the office building and site entrance. I instinctively kept low, and from my vantage point I saw at least four men rush into the office. Others went into the timber chalets on either side of the grassed centre of the site, and others started examining the bikes parked around.

I played safe. I turned off my camping stove, grabbed my wallet containing all my papers and took off into the surrounding woods.

After an hour I was beginning to doubt that I had done the right thing, and decided to creep back and take a look. This almost proved my undoing, as just in time I spotted three men around my tent. One was going through my belongings. They wrote something in their notebooks, shrugged at each other and went back to the office.

I stayed where I was, because from this new position I could see the site and all that was happening. Suddenly there was a shrill blast on a whistle. All the visitors returned to their cars and swept out of the camp at speed, just as it had been described to me the previous day.

Vaclav and the other organisers looked shaken but, by now resigned to the system, assured us it was normal and that we should not worry. We - and I speak for all - were not worried for ourselves, but for any action that the authorities would take against our hosts once we had departed. Such was their desire to have us keep coming, and to be able to maintain contact with the West, that it overcame even a visit from the secret police.

Chapter Twenty
SWEDEN 1979

In a complete change for 1979, Lil and I headed for Harwich and the ship to Göteborg. Also for a change, we were aboard the BSA and Palma.

We rolled off the ship and followed the traffic up to the customs post, where an officer asked to see my passport. He looked through it slowly and then, to my astonishment, asked me to go with him to the office. Lil was left sitting in the sidecar wondering what was going on, and I found myself facing three Swedish customs men sat at a desk. They too looked carefully at my passport. By now I was thinking that perhaps it was out of date, but then they asked me, 'Why do you go to so many Eastern European countries, and so often?' To see my friends, I replied, which is the same reason that I come to Sweden now.

Why they suddenly queried my passport or my intentions I have no idea. By 1979 I had visited Sweden at least six times without any question. But they assured me it was just a routine question, welcomed me to the country and hoped I would have a happy visit.

Lil and I visited many friends, some of whom I had met at rallies in Czechoslovakia. The 650 Thunderbolt proved an ideal machine for Sweden, with its lovely main roads and its dirt connecting roads. Yes, I mean dirt. They become grooved and rutted by heavy lorries, and when it rains, boy do you and the bike get in a mess.

I found that the best way to negotiate them was fairly fast, about forty-five or fifty miles any hour, when the outfit would tend to skim over the surface and so give a smoother ride. Apparently the surfaces are sprayed with an oil and rolled to stabilise them, but they took some getting used to.

However, the BSA coped well and gave no trouble, still managing to return around sixty miles to the gallon. The only problem was the much-muddied underside of the Palma, and its low-slung fog lamp took a bit of a battering.

What I do like about Swedish highways is the system of under-taking (not the terminal one). You are riding along, you glance in the mirror and see someone closing on you, so you simply pull over to the right into the lane provided. The vehicle passes by without needing to change lanes and then, when the lane is clear again, you pull back into it.

The SMC, the Swedish Riders' organisation, has some enviable facilities. Our friends took us to the lovely lakeside camp they have in Jönköping. It was specially built for them and we were made very welcome. There was a well-stocked bar in the luxurious clubhouse, plenty of camping space under the trees or at the lakeside, and the opportunity to go boating if we wished. It was very pleasant to be able to take Lil, and to visit places without having to worry about whether she would be upset by meeting hostile secret policemen or stony-faced border guards.

Chapter Twenty One
GERMANY, POLAND AND CZECHOSLOVAKIA 1980

This was to be an involved trip, taking, taking in three Eastern Bloc countries, so much form-filling was necessary during the months leading up to my take-off. One of the reasons was to enable me to attend the Scorpion Rally, held near Warsaw, so careful planning was needed as I had so many borders to cross.

Finally I was able to load up my G80 with presents for friends, a few Norton and Matchless spares, plus my own luggage, clothes and camping gear. I set the rear tyre at forty pounds pressure, checked all my visas and accompanying paperwork one last time, and rode through the night to Ramsgate.

I took the first hovercraft, at 6.30 a.m., and less than an hour later I was riding away from Calais. The weather was dry and all was well as I rode through Dunkerque, Gent, Antwerp, Nijmegen, Arnhem, Hanover, and on towards Berlin. I chose this as a change from my usual route. I also had a plan in mind that would save me some time, although it did have its hazards.

Arriving once more at the entrance to the 'corridor' at Marienborn, I was despatched in the direction of Berlin. But a few miles out of Berlin, where the motorway swings south near Potsdam, I came upon just what I had been looking for. Some heavy lorries were also heading south. I sneaked in on the inside of the convoy, hidden from the military observation post at the motorway junction. With my heart in my mouth, I kept pace with the lorries and was soon heading east, well clear of the control points.

This meant that I could carry on without being held up at the infamous Checkpoint Charlie. Soon I was on the outskirts of the city and started to head north, so as to enter Berlin from the east. This may sound complicated, but was actually straightforward, and soon I had found Gunter's home and was settled down with him and his wife Monica, making plans for the next day's run to Warsaw.

We left Gunter's house early the next morning and were soon on the road to Frankfurt an der Oder and the Polish border, me on the G80 and him on a rather hard-working 250cc MZ, a single-cylinder two-stroke. The sun was coming out and I was looking forward to a good ride, followed by an evening with old friends.

Then it all started to go wrong. We rode up to the East German border post. I had to enter a lane for non-nationals, Gunter another lane running parallel with mine. The typical unsmiling guard closely examined my passport and visa, then rather surprised me by prodding me with his sub-machine gun into the control office. Here, several guard officers held what seemed a minute examination of my papers and then demanded to know how I proposed to leave Poland. I showed them my Czech visa. This seemed to annoy them, as I think they hoped my papers were not in order.

Then, with an exclamation almost of joy, one of the guards said, 'Ha! You are in big trouble! You did not get your visa signed when you stayed in Berlin yesterday.' He was quite right, I did not. But I had been in Berlin for only twenty hours, and it plainly said, as I pointed out, that I must report to the police only if I stayed anywhere for twenty-four hours or more. My visa was stamped at Marienborn at nine o'clock the previous evening. It was now eight in the morning. I pointed this out to him as well.

He exploded. I wondered for a moment if he was going to hit me, but he just pushed me down on a chair before all three of them and disappeared with my papers. Wait, I must wait.

After about an hour they returned, seemingly a lot more pleasant, and took me outside to where my G80 was still resting on its stand. I looked across to the lane which Gunter had taken. I saw that his MZ had had its luggage removed, and then Gunter appeared flanked by two guards. He was then stood so that I could see him and I was asked, 'Is this the man you stayed with in Berlin?' I said that it was adding that I had reported to his street controller in Berlin, who would confirm what I was saying. This seemed to satisfy them and they ordered me to stand by my machine.

More time passed, and then a guard came out and gave me back my passport and papers and signalled me to go. I started up and rode out of the lane, into the short strip of no man's land between the border posts. Looking back I saw no sign of Gunter, so I waited until he appeared at last.

It was not until we had passed through the Polish border post, which took only half an hour, that I was able to find out what had happened. Gunter had been subjected to a great deal of questioning and a body search, and the guards had also gone through his entire luggage. He had been told that he was a very bad German and should not have encouraged me to visit. He told them a lie. He said that he had not known I was coming, but had turned up by chance.

This was the danger in crossing a border with a friend. There was always the chance that you would be separated and asked questions. Naturally, the guards would be comparing my answers with those of my friend and hoping to find inconsistencies. It could become quite an absorbing game: what would they be asking Gunter, what would he be saying, what questions would he be expecting them to ask of me, and so on.

I have to say that, whether travelling on my own or in company, I set no great store by telling the truth on these occasions. It was best to stick mostly to the facts, because it was simpler to do so and because some of them could be checked. I always took the view that my main objective was to cross the border, and I would say whatever I had to say in order to do so. I viewed their entire political system as a great big lie, so felt that telling a border guard one or two little ones was justifiable.

It was noon by this time. Although it was early June, the wind swept across the bleak open countryside and it was quite cold. We rode on through Poznan, Kutno, and with some careful navigating by Gunter we arrived at the campsite in the forest of Buda Grabski, just this side of Warsaw.

What a welcome we received! It is difficult to describe accurately just what a feeling I got on these occasions. It was always such a sincere greeting, and they would say how pleased they were that somebody in the free West had taken the trouble to come.

'Taking the trouble' was an appropriate expression. The work and worry to get the visas, the complications of working out a route, the border hostility - yes, it did mean taking some trouble. But the sincerity of the greeting would immediately wash it all away. These inconveniences could then be seen in their true perspective.

There were several other Western riders there, from Sweden, Germany, Denmark and the Netherlands, but most were Polish and Czech. The bikes varied from Honda, Suzuki, BMW and the like from the West, to the Czech CZs and Simsons and a couple of BMWs from the 1930s. Much vodka, slivovitz and beer flowed, and I was kept busy supplying the answers regarding motorcycling in Britain.

One the things I had brought with me was for a friend I met at the rally; a complete clutch for a pre-war Norton Inter with the AMC gearbox, plus a few other odds and ends. I also dug deep into my supply of stickers and badges and distributed them as liberally as I could. Not only was there the pleasure of giving on these occasions, but also the thought of the weight reduction when I next loaded up the bike! However, goods were also passing in the other direction. On the second and final day of the rally, I was honoured by being presented with a beautiful cup for being the furthest-travelled visitor. I still treasure it.

I left with the main Czechoslovakian contingent, saying goodbye to Gunter at this point. We rode south via Piotrków, Czestochowa and Katowice to the border at Cieszyn. The Czechs had only to show their travel permits and they were waved through, crossing the bridge spanning the River Olse and waiting for me on the Czech side. I prepared myself for the usual rigmarole.

There then followed the only pleasant and trouble-free border crossing I ever had in all my Eastern Bloc travels, before or since. A charming Polish border guard took me completely by surprise when he saw the bike I was riding. 'Matchless, Matchless!' he exclaimed, shaking me by the hand. He called out an equally charming young lady guard, who also went through the exclaiming and hand-shaking business. Then she ran back to the control building and re-emerged waving some photographs.

There were two photos: an old Matchless G3 and an AJS model 18 of about 1954 vintage. 'Ours,' they said. 'We have them in Katowice.' And with that they fell to their knees to give the G80 a very close inspection. Eventually I almost had to insist that they had a look at my passport and stamped my visa. I found some stickers and badges to give them, which added to their delight and gave me great pleasure too.

The Czechs watching me from across the river were amazed at the sight of it all, and when I finally joined them it took some explaining. They quite thought that the guards were friends of mine.

I carried on to Gottwaldov and the home of Vaclav and his family. Spending a few days in this more eastern part of Czechoslovakia, we rode around and called on some of his friends, most of them motorcyclists as well. A lot more of this wonderful country was revealed tome, and I saw many old Czech machines: Praga, Jawa, Premier and CZ. Not all the Jawas were the rather primitive two-strokes which we see in Britain. I was given the opportunity to ride a 500cc OHC single-cylinder Jawa by one of Vaclav's friends, a very neat machine with impressive performance.

Finally setting of for home once again, I headed for Brno and the north road to Prague. This route, which by 1980 I had ridden many times, took me near the town of Kutná Hóra, and just a few miles from there is a village called Malin.

It was here that I made an interesting discovery. On a small hill is a collection of stones to mark the site of a wartime tragedy. An inscription plate says that a German officer and a number of soldiers lie buried there. I was examining this plate when a local farmer appeared, greeting me in German. Once we had sorted out my nationality, he asked if I knew what I was looking at.

He told me the story. During the 1939-45 war, the Red Army was breaking out and advancing across Czechoslovakia with the Germans in full retreat. On this little hill, a young officer and his platoon were holding up the advance. They were hopelessly outnumbered, and the Soviet army offered them safe conduct if they surrendered. It has to be, and the officer agreed to spare the unnecessary deaths of his men. When they had handed over their weapons they were all killed on the spot. As far as I could make out, local people had erected the memorial and buried the dead. I could only take the farmer at his word, although for some reason I did believe him.

It reminded me of another tale I was told, by a Czech who was present at the scene of an act of revenge against the Germans in Prague. The Special Operations Executive in Britain planned it with the Czechs. Some nationals who had escaped to Britain were dropped by parachute and carried out the assassination of the Gestapo chief, Reinhard Heydrich.

In Prague I stayed once again with Frank and Jana and their two boys, having entered the city via the Mala Strana and Soviet Tanske Square, then into the busy city street of Kirovova, which by this time felt entirely familiar.

The next day I decided to make use of my usual tours of the city on foot. I crossed over the River Vitavo that divides the city and kept a lookout for any shop windows displaying bohemian crystal glass. On each of my visits to Prague I made a point of buying a piece, and a traditional doll to take home to Lil. I had my usual look around Prague Castle, seat of the present government, and the beautiful Wenceslas cathedral. Nobody followed me this time. Maybe they had finally realised that it was just me, and nothing to do with MI5.

I also had to report to the aliens' office, as I was to stay for three days. Entering the building, I searched out the appropriate form and sat down to fill it in.

I then became aware of American voices close to me, and overheard a young couple discussing their bewilderment at all the documentation. They made their way to a door, knocked on it and went into a room off the main hall. Five minutes later, just as I completed my paperwork, they emerged looking even more lost. The young lady was crying by this time. Her companion tried to console her, and by chance they sat down next to me. The man said to her that if only someone there could speak English, they could understand what the problem was. The temptation was too great: I turned to him and asked if I could help.

I must say that I get a lot of fun out of giving people harmless shocks in this way, but he recovered quickly and went through their story. 'They say our visa is not correct but don't explain why. Nobody smiles, nobody will speak so I can understand, my wife is distressed.'

I asked to see the visa. I could see at once that it was a transit visa, requiring them to be out of the country by the end of that day. They had planned to spend a few days in Prague, having driven there from Germany, and had obviously been given the wrong visa in the US.

I told them that I could take them to the US Embassy, as I knew where it was, and there they could start going about having their visa extended and the confusion cleared up. But they didn't have much time, because after midnight they would be in the country illegally. By this time they were looking frightened. They had already fallen foul of the police on the road and were shocked by their treatment since entering Czechoslovakia. They looked like that had had enough of the country.

So I advised them to leave and gave them the quickest route out of the country. I warned them of the strict speed controls and the military zones, and I told them to take it steady but not to stop. They had the rest of the day to get back to Germany, which was plenty of time if they got started straight away. They thanked me and left.

This all made me wonder if the various East European embassies in Western Countries were giving enough information to help travellers. This American couple knew neither what they were holding, nor what they needed.

The next day Frank and I visited a friend of his who lived on the Prague Plzen road and had lots of old motorbikes. Although he and Frank knew each other, he was most suspicious of me. He had bikes everywhere - leaning against trees in an old orchard, in sheds, some just parked in groups out in the open. I would have liked to have spent some time examining them and talking to him, but I could see that he wasn't keen on the idea, and neither were his three Doberman dogs. But I did spot at least one Norton 16H and what I think was an Ariel VH.

Talking of Ariels, Frank owns quite a few of them, along with many spares. Originally he kept them in his old, large flat in Kirovova. But then he, Jana and family had to leave owing to the danger of subsidence. A new line was being built on the

Prague metro, and the tunnelling caused cracks to appear in the walls of the old apartment building.

Frank had known the Ariel Importer in Prague. I'm not sure when the last bikes arrived there from the factory in Birmingham; maybe around 1960. Frank eventually bought the dealer's last machine from his widow: an old 600cc VB sidevalve.

After three days I left, the motorcycle parts in my luggage replaced by cut glass and other gifts. I rode to Rozvodov and had the usual ninety-minute border crossing, followed by a run up to Aachen and my usual campsite near the city centre. The site is easy to find and ideal for anyone in transit, whether it be for Belgium, the Netherlands or Germany, as it is placed near the junction of these borders.

The next day I rode to Calais, took the hovercraft to Ramsgate and then rode the final three hundred miles to my home in Devon. A day or two later I started doing some arithmetic on a piece of scrap paper, and thinking over my years with the Matchless G80. It was now twenty-five years old. This latest trip had put another 3,900 miles on the clock, and the bike had now covered a total of 125,000 miles.

Since buying it, and other than routine adjustments, the only maintenance I had carried out had been two decokes and the fitting of new piston rings at 80,000 miles. I had removed and cleaned the magneto and dynamo once, re-greased all the bearings once, and fitted new primary and drive chains. The bottom end of the engine was untouched. I can get around 30,000 miles from a tyre on this bike, and it had probably used about ten spark plugs. Excluding oil and petrol, I reckoned that the Matchless had cost me less than £300 over all those miles. I'm not complaining.

Chapter Twenty Two
BERLIN 1981

I wanted to visit Gunter and Monica in East Berlin again. My mind was made up when I received an invitation from a friend from my village in Devon, and who was working at the British Embassy in West Berlin. I was invited to stay for a night in Churchill House (a large accommodation building for British people working in West Berlin it appeared, both for Military andEmbassy Staff.) I decided to visit both sides of the city.

I took my usual route: Dover, across to Calais, Dunkerque, Lille, Aachen, Cologne, Dortmund, Hanover, and the border at Helmstedt. Here is the entrance to the infamous corridor to the inland island of West Berlin, and where the realities of twentieth-century European politics give the system a severe jolt.

I rode the G80 gently to the checkpoint and surrendered my passport, visa and papers for the bike. As usual at an Eastern Block border control, no help or information was offered. A traveller needs patience and an instinct to interpret whatever might arise. After a few questions and an hour's wait, I was allowed past.

As always when riding along the corridor, I was given a time by which I must arrive at the West Berlin border, one hundred and ten miles away. I saw that I had been given two and three-quarter hours, requiring me to average forty miles an hour. If I were not to appear at the other end at that time, or even if I were to be late, they would be out looking for me and I would be in trouble. But with the Matchless going well, I made it in two and a half hours and started going through the paperwork and answering questions all over again.

After another hour I was in West Berlin, trying to follow the hand-drawn map which my host had given me. I found Churchill House, parked, and announced my arrival into the speaker unit by the door.

My friend's plan was to give me a quick sightseeing tour of the western part of the city, so an interesting afternoon and evening speedily went by. At one stage we were close to the Wall and I could plainly see the tall tower in Alexanderplatz in the Eastern sector. I remarked that I would be on the other side of the Wall the following day, and in a completely different atmosphere.

An idea was forming in my mind as I spoke - or maybe it was seeing the Brandenberg Gate from the Western side. I began to wonder if I could cross into East Berlin via an 'unauthorised' crossing point, intended for German citizens with special permits only. The idea took hold. Next morning I left Churchill House heading east, then rode parallel with the Wall, looking down each street that led to the barrier.

I must explain that where the Wall had been built across a street, all the houses on the eastern side within about fifty yards of it had been demolished to leave an open space. This was to deprive any would-be escapees of any cover. Thus I was able to see the guard towers situated at frequent intervals along the Wall's length - which also meant that the guards in the towers could see me. At each one I saw binoculars trained on me.

At last I found one of the crossing points. I turned into the street and rode slowly up to the barrier, the Matchless engine thumping quietly. It was overlooked by a pulpit-like tower from which an unsmiling guard stared down. I did my best to assume an honest and appealing expression and looked up at him for a long time. He looked back, not moving a muscle.

After what seemed like an age, but which I later estimated had been ten minutes, he pushed a button to lift the barrier. I rode forward, the bike having been idling all this time, and on to the guard at the control building. He looked incredulously at me, then held out his hand for my papers. Calling for support, he was joined by two shaken-looking colleagues. On spotting my GB plate they went into a huddle, then ordered me off the bike and marched me into their office.

What, why and where from, they demanded. I put on an even more honest and appealing expression as I played the innocent. Eventually they left me sitting in an office while they phoned some distant authority. They made me wait for an hour or so, then marched me back to the bike and pointed me back the way I had come. I selected an expression of mild surprise, then nodded and set about starting my bike once again.

I rode back to the first barrier and my old friend in his lofty perch. We went through the same humourless encounter as before. For at least ten minutes by Matchless thumped away, until, unsmiling and indeed betraying no emotion whatever, he released me back into the West. I rode past the barrier and headed for Checkpoint Charlie.

Chapter Twenty Three
CZECHOSLOVAKIA AND POLAND 1982

In 1969 I had bought a six-year old AJS 350. I had been able to find out that the bottom end of the engine had not been touched since it left the factory, but that owing to some sort of misuse the cylinder barrel had been rebored to +0.040 inches. I completely stripped the engine and examined everything. The big end and main bearings were perfect but I renewed the timing side bush, fitted new piston rings and did my usual tidying-up job on the cylinder head ports.

The Matchless Company had bought AJS in 1931 and the two model ranges had moved steadily closer after that. By 1963, only a few years before production ended, an AJS 350 was almost identical to a Matchless 350. But the single-cylinder engine had been redesigned the previous year, ostensibly to give more power. In everyday use I have never found any significant difference between the old design and the new, but the newer one is faster - I have had well over eighty miles an hour out of this particular machine. But speed is not what I'm after. Reliability and economy are the essential things, and the AJS has given me just that for many years.

Vaclav and Frank had heard me talk about this bike, and had asked me to leave the G80 at home one year and use the AJS instead. I said I would, intending to do so only once. As it turned out, I used it for every subsequent East European trip.

I made all my usual preparations and then loaded the little 350cc to capacity, or maybe a little more: clothes, camping and cooking gear, tinned food, tea and coffee, motorcycle parts, presents. I took the hovercraft as usual, disembarked at Calais and rode to Waidhaus, almost on the Czech border.

This was a good point to evaluate the performance of the AJS. Leaving home at ten o'clock on Friday night, I had ridden straight to Dover, taken the first hovercraft on Saturday morning, then ridden virtually non-stop to my camping point. It was then nine o'clock on Saturday evening, and I had put seven hundred and sixty miles on the bike's odometer since leaving home. Cruising at fifty-five to sixty miles an hour, fuel consumption was better than eighty to the gallon and I was able to cover over three hundred miles between fuel stops. Mind you, my backside at that time was probably one of the hardest in Europe.

I pitched my tent using the light from the headlamp, feeling very confident about the days ahead with my new tourer.

The border at Rozvodov seemed unusually active, and with the usual 'Good Luck!' shout to me from the West German guards I rolled up to the Czech border. There must have been some sort of trouble or problem there not long before as they were even more surly than usual. I guessed then that ~I would be held up for some time, and it took two hours and a lot of talking before they cleared me and the AJS and I could ride slowly towards the 'inner control' and into Czechoslovakia proper.

Arriving at Prague, I was caught up in heavy traffic near some traffic lights. I found myself alongside a GB-plated car, its driver studying a street map of the city as we waited for the lights to change. It was a three-litre Rover, I remember.

As with the American couple two years before, I couldn't resist the opportunity of giving him a start. His window was wound down, so I leaned across and asked him if he wanted directions. He nearly jumped out of his skin on hearing an English voice, but then recovered and told me he was looking for the British Embassy, and had been for over an hour.

I told him to follow me closely, put the AJS in gear and drew in front of him. Eventually I was able to lead him to the embassy, where I pulled up and we talked for a while. He seemed intrigued by my having ridden such a heavily laden bike there. It was so unusual to find another British registered vehicle behind the Iron Curtain that I much enjoyed our rather inconsequential chat.

By this time I had been visiting Eastern Europe for the best part of ten years. I had made many visits to Czechoslovakia, Poland, Hungary, Romania and East Germany. I believe that I had been able to piece together a reasonably representative picture of life for ordinary people behind the Iron Curtain, and I cannot recall ever having regretted putting myself through all the bureaucracy and border unpleasantness.

One thing that almost everyone I met told me was how much they valued the BBC World Service broadcasts. They tuned in on radios hidden under floorboards and really did believe that the BBC would give them all the facts. One old Czech man of eighty told me that, if the BBC said that tomorrow the moon would be blue, and then if on the morrow it was white, then he would know that the Russians had painted it. Such was their faith.

This sounds strange now, but in those days, behind the Curtain, truth was hard to find and news from the West hard to come by. Hearing that they would tune in to the BBC as a first choice, and at some personal risk, I always took as an enormous compliment.

A few days later I was heading for Gottwaldov again, this time taking a different route through Svitavy, Olomouc, Prerov and so to Gottwaldov and Hovezi, and the now so familiarly camp-site. I had another great time amongst my European and Scandinavian friends, but when I left camp this time I headed for Ostrava and into Poland. After a comparatively speedy one-hour crossing I rode up to Wroclaw, Bydgoszcz and on to the Baltic port of Gdansk. I called on a friend, and then after dark I rode to the border near Szczecin, continuing on to the French coast via Bremen, Amsterdam and Brugge.

Unfortunately, I had little time for exploring, but at least this hectic schedule enabled me to put the AJS through its paces. I camped twice after leaving Gdansk but had averaged just over four hundred miles a day, trying to do at least some sight-seeing. The bike ran marvellously and my smuggled Polish and East German money saw me through. By the time I finally rode up the hill to my home I was convinced of the prowess of the AJS. I had covered over 3,800 miles in ten days, riding on all but two of them.

Chapter Twenty Four
WHEN THE WALL
CAME DOWN

By the mid-1980s, I was reflecting more and more on all my journeys to Eastern Europe. Why was I doing it? Did it really benefit anybody? Was it becoming repetitive? With experience, was it in turn becoming the 'safe' touring destination I had sought to escape in 1974?

Then I would think about all the differences between life here and life there, and this would reassure me that it had been worthwhile. Take, for instance, the simple matter of choice in almost every kind of shop there: very limited, often poor quality, and usually a scarcity of meat, fish and fresh fruit. I remembered a queue I had seen in Warsaw, hundreds of yards long, for bananas. I am sure that had it been possible to transport an ordinary Czech or Pole or Hungarian straight over here and into my ordinary local supermarket, he would not have believed his eyes.

Travel itself is the other big difference. The fact that virtually nobody could leave these countries, the lack of news and information, the jamming of Western radio broadcasts and the severe penalties imposed on anyone who tried to take newspapers or magazines across the border all added up to a feeling of hopelessness and frustration.

I would always conclude these reflections by deciding once again that all the inconvenience, paperwork and necessary fortitude to pass over the borders was truly worthwhile. It gave me a feeling that visiting countries of the free world could not give, and it always seemed such a pity that more people did not take up the challenge. Now they will never know.

I really cannot say that all was universal misery behind the Iron Curtain. But with the everyday frustrations, with the secret police and incessant propaganda, with the low standards of living, life could resemble an assault course.

Can there be such a thing as a national consciousness? What happens exactly when, after forty-five years of arbitrary division people decide they have had enough? Sitting watching my TV in the final weeks of 1989, seeing pictures of hundreds of people of East Berlin straddling the infamous Wall, laughing and cheering as they smashed it to pieces with hammers and iron bars, I could barely believe it was true. At the very least, I kept expecting to hear gunfire as the guards came to their senses.

So many times I had stood near the Brandenberg Gate. On the Western side I had been within fifty yards of the graffiti-covered wall. On the East, armed guards and towers kept me at least a hundred yards away. Now it seemed that soon I would be able to walk beneath the Gate.

I remembered how I had stopped at the foot of the Wall in the East and watched young people dancing to music coming from Western rock bands playing concerts on the other side. They couldn't see them but they could certainly hear them. That is probably my most poignant memory of all.

But I also remember the great celebrations in East Berlin in 1987, marking the 750th anniversary of the founding of the city. The great procession that passed down Karl Marx Allee took over four hours, and the marshalling of such an extraordinary spectacle surpassed anything that was organised in West Berlin. When I returned home nobody in Britain knew anything about it, but I am sure I shall never see anything like it again.

The day after the main event, I was invited to ride in the back seat of a Hermann Goering type of open Mercedes-Benz driven amongst the masses in Alexanderplatz by a very refined lady wearing a large brimmed hat. It was like a dream: hundreds of miles from home, waving from my superior position to the excited though orderly crowds. I wonder who they thought I was.

Soon after the Wall was demolished, my postman delivered an invitation to the first 'free' motorcycle rally to be held in east (rather than East) Berlin. It was being organised by my friend in Berlin in co-operation with a West German motorcycle club, and was open to all.

I quickly made my plan. I would attend, and afterwards I would make my way south to Prague. In the event, by the date of the rally Czechoslovakia too was free, at least as far as border controls of the old type. I advertised the event as widely as I could in Britain, as I wanted to do all I could to ensure it success.

A few weeks later, AJS fully loaded, I set out for Dover. I had decided to head for a border crossing point at which I had suffered much frustration in the past: the Hamburg to Berlin north transit route.

As I neared the border control point, which is quite massive in area, I slowed almost to walking pace. Before me loomed the first building, but no longer did it seem ominous. The road had been cleared of the width-restricting barriers, there was nobody in sight and the doors were closed. It was eerie. In the silence and the emptiness, I realised that I was actually feeling lonely.

I should by now have been brought fiercely to a halt, had my passport and visa snatched away, and been made to stand away from my bike and wait. After half an hour, I should have been made to push my bike to the next control, where more paperwork inspections and questions would follow. Then another push to the exchange bank, where I would be oblige to sell sterling for about one-fifth of its value on any street corner once inside the country. Then more pushing to the final check-point before finally being released into East Germany.

Instead, incredibly, there I was slowly thumping my way forward, on the main transit road and in a state of disbelief. Any moment now a guard would shout at me or shoot at me. But nothing happened; absolutely nothing. I thought about all my previous border crossings and all of a sudden I was almost in tears. I wrenched open the throttle and accelerated away.

I continued along the familiar road, swinging south and entering the city and the home of my friends. Here I learned something odd: the East German Mark was still the currency, but was being used alongside the Western Deutschmark. They were supposedly of equal value but some unscrupulous businessman and officials were operating an exchange rate of two and a half to one. Later I even found that this was more or less an official exchange rate - rather a strange way to re-introduce East Germany to the free world.

A much more ominous warning was also given to me. I should now be very careful where I parked my bike and should leave no luggage unattended on it, even for a few minutes. This quite shook me, as I had found in virtually every Communist-controlled country that I need have no worries about theft.

So just what had I discovered? Now they were free, it meant not only that they could travel if they had the money to do so. But now the criminal pollution of the West was upon them. The umbrella of the Communist regime had gone and they were as exposed as we were.

Don't think for a moment that I started having second thoughts about Communism. But here was something that I had never considered or had reason to consider.

What a sight it was, seeing riders from the West arriving as freely and easily as if it had been a rally in Britain. There were a few arguments when it became obvious that currency rates were subject to variable interpretation according to the person involved, but no rider I talked to even mentioned the border crossings! They did not realise how easy it had been. I had the feeling that some thought I had exaggerated or even made up some of my tales about border guards, but then they hadn't seen it for themselves.

It felt like the end of an era, and I had so many memories to conjure in my mind that weekend. How grateful I was towards my reliable Matchless, AJS and BSA machines that had enabled me to travel safely and confidently behind the Iron Curtain, and on so many other journeys. To have ridden up to frontiers to be challenged and often humiliated. To have met the ordinary people in their troubled state and subdued way of life. To have seen their faces and felt their gratitude when I was able to give them spare parts, magazines, even little luxuries like scented soap - this made it worthwhile.

Chapter Twenty Five
LAST THOUGHTS

Surely the motorcycle was the ideal mode of transport in such times and such circumstances. A car would have been too easily spotted and challenged or even impounded. My bike could be easily hidden - and was, sometimes - and also enable me to take roads that would have been impassable in a car. Just to be able to cover eighty miles on a gallon of petrol was valuable, given the scarcity of petrol stations and the uncertainty of their having any supplies anyway.

The simple engineering used to design and build the bikes I rode was also an advantage. Had I been unlucky enough to suffer a major failure a long way from home, it would not have been such a disaster as on a sophisticated modern machine. It would have been just a matter of stripping the bike and enlisting the help at a local engineering works.

Often, however, when I met riders in the more remote parts of Eastern Europe, they quite thought that my 1955 Matchless and 1963 AJS were the latest British motorcycles and were not at all impressed by the journey I had made. They were unaware that by the mid-1970s, the British motorcycle manufacturing scene had all but ebbed away. It was only when

121

fellow riders from Sweden, the Netherlands and West Germany penetrated the Iron Curtain on their modern machines that they knew the truth.

But then, I am admittedly biased towards British bikes. My maybe old-fashioned ways showed up strongly with all my attendances at FIM Rallies - always on a British bike. I thought I would best represent my country at each rally's Parade of Nations by riding one of its products.

I also became quite convinced that engine size did not matter much when choosing a touring motorcycle. How often I was asked by prospective touring riders what machine I used, and how surprised they were to learn that I was not using at least a 750cc bike, or even a fairly new one. Any lingering doubts I had on this score were dispelled when I changed from my 500 Matchless to my 350 AJS for my jaunts.

Preparation is the key. I took care over my bike, luggage gear, the luggage itself, tent and general camping gear, and of course all the documentation. Taking what I needed, and maximising the reliability of all that I took, was of far more value and saved far more time than rapid acceleration or high top speeds.

I mentioned my 1939 Ariel in the chapter on Scotland. I have used this little bike, and even my 1932 Matchless and sidecar, on foreign tours as well - particularly to France. The outfit, although very slow by modern standards, was also extremely reliable. Lil often said that the old pram-type springing in the sidecar made it more comfortable than the much newer Palma attached to the BSA.

Naturally, over a touring lifetime of nearly fifty years, I met all sorts of people on my travels. While motorcycling changed completely during that time, I never really met a rider that I disliked. A few weren't my type, but most seemed to think and so much the same as me.

Perhaps in all those years, the riders I ended up admiring the most were the members of the Four-Stroke Motorcycle Club in Czechoslovakia. In the absence of dealer networks, maintenance manuals and spare parts, their enthusiasm was second to none and the ingenuity they employed in order to keep their bikes on the road had to be seen to be believed.

I am so glad that I was able to help these riders, many of whom became great friends. How easy it was for me in Britain to locate virtually any part I wanted! So, the weight of spares that I usually carried as I headed east - engine halves, gearboxes, clutches, even wheel rims slung over a shoulder - never felt like a burden. As I travelled, I would get great pleasure from thinking about those spares, and my friends' faces when I handed them over.

Now, with travel and access so easy to nearly all European countries, and as I continue to ride my motorcycles abroad and to visit my friends, I hope I will be joined by many other riders from Britain and beyond. After all, what could be better than to be able to travel, without let or hindrance?

INDEX

A

B

I

J

K

L

M

R

S

T